Nourishing the Essence of Life

Nourishing the Essence of Life

THE OUTER, INNER, AND SECRET
TEACHINGS OF TAOISM

Translated with an introduction by
Eva Wong

SHAMBHALA
Boston & London 2004

Shambhala Publications, Inc.
Horticultural Hall
300 Massachusetts Avenue
Boston, Massachusetts 02115
www.shambhala.com

9 8 7 6 5 4 3 2 1

First Edition

Printed in the United States of America

Library of Congress Cataloging-in-Publication Data

Nourishing the essence of life: the outer, inner, and secret teachings of Taoism /
Translated with an introduction by Eva Wong.—1st ed.
p.   cm.
Uniform title not available.
ISBN 1-59030-104-8 (pbk.: alk. paper)
1. Taoism.   I. Title: Outer, inner, and secret teachings of Taoism.
II. Wong, Eva, 1951–
BL1920.N68   2004
299′.514—dc21
2003013553

Contents

I   TRANSLATOR'S
INTRODUCTION

Tao-hsüan p'ien   25   THE MYSTERIES
OF THE TAO

Wu-hsüan p'ien   49   UNDERSTANDING
THE MYSTERIES

T'ai-hsüan pao-tien   71   THE SACRED TREATISE
ON THE GREAT MYSTERY

Nourishing the Essence of Life

Translator's Introduction

This book contains translations of three texts on understanding the Tao in the macrocosm of the universe and the microcosm of the body: the *Tao-hsüan p'ien* (The Mysteries of the Tao), the *Wu-hsüan p'ien* (Understanding the Mysteries), and the *T'ai-hsüan pao-tien* (The Sacred Treatise on the Great Mystery). All three texts are found in the *T'ai-hsüan* section of the Taoist canon, and all are texts from the tradition of the Ch'üan-chen (Complete Reality) school of Taoism.

The *Tao-hsüan p'ien* was written by Wang Tao sometime between the end of the Yüan (1271–1368) and the beginning of the Ming (1368–1644) dynasties. This text contains teachings common to both the northern and southern branches of the Complete Reality school. The *Wu-hsüan p'ien* and *T'ai-hsüan pao-tien* are texts of the southern branch and contain teachings that are particular to that school.

I chose these texts for this volume for two reasons. First, I believe that together they form an excellent introduction to the three levels of Taoist teachings—outer, inner, and secret—within one lineage of transmission, the Complete Reality tradition. Second, I want to introduce the teachings of southern

Complete Reality Taoism, a school whose teachings are relatively unknown among the noninitiates of internal alchemical Taoism.

Outer, Inner, and Secret Teachings of Taoism

Outer teachings are intended for a general audience and novice practitioners: they are easy to understand and can be studied and practiced without a teacher's supervision. Inner teachings are intended for practitioners who have built the necessary spiritual foundation for deeper practice. These teachings are more esoteric, and the texts are designed to supplement formal instruction from a teacher. Secret teachings are the most advanced; they are intended for the highest adepts and are transmitted orally, directly from teacher to student. Texts of secret teachings are intended as notes to help the student remember the teacher's instructions. Armchair enthusiasts of Taoism can understand intellectually the three levels of teachings given the appropriate background information, but practitioners must receive supervision from a teacher of a lineage before practicing the inner and secret teachings. Therefore, the *Tao-hsüan p'ien* and the *T'ai-hsüan pao-tien* should not be used as manuals of Taoist training without guidance from a qualified teacher.

The Northern and Southern Complete Reality Schools

The Complete Reality school is divided into southern and northern branches. The teachings of southern Complete Reality Taoism are less systematic and more difficult to follow than those of the northern branch. This is because the southern branch was always a lay tradition consisting of a loosely knit group of practitioners spread over a large area of southern China, while the northern branch is a tightly knit monastic organization that has maintained continuity from its founding in the thirteenth century to the present day. The southern school was nominally led by a patriarch, but in reality the followers trained under autonomous teachers. Even today the lineage of this school is carried by a handful of independent teachers. In contrast, the northern Complete Reality school maintains a large network of monasteries and temples throughout the world and has a standardized curriculum of study and practice.

Although Chang Po-tuan of the northern Sung dynasty (960–1126) is recognized as the founder of southern Complete Reality Taoism, the division between the northern and southern branches occurred during the time of Chang's teacher Liu Hai-ch'an. Both Liu Hai-ch'an and Wang Ch'ung-yang studied under Lü Tung-pin of the late T'ang (618–906). While Wang was strongly influenced by Ch'an (Zen) Buddhism and Confucianism and advocated the cultivation of mind before body, Liu favored the practices of sexual alchemy and advocated the cultivation of body before mind. By the time Chang Po-tuan received the teachings from Liu Hai-ch'an, and Ch'iu Ch'ang-ch'un received the transmission from Wang Ch'ung-yang, the southern and northern branches of the Complete Reality school were recognized officially as separate lineages.

Although the two branches shared similarities in advocating the dual cultivation of body and mind, several major differences exist between them. First, the northern branch placed more importance on cultivating the mind and taught that mind must be cultivated before the body. The southern branch placed more importance on strengthening the body and focused on gathering, refining, and circulating internal energy. Second, the northern school does not use sexual techniques for gathering energy, while for the southern school, sexual yoga is a viable method for replenishing energy in the early stages of training, especially for older practitioners. Third, as a non-temple-based lineage, the southern branch did not have the elaborate ceremonies and rituals that are integral to northern Complete Reality Taoism. Last, more variations in theory and practice exist among the practitioners of the southern school than the northern school. This is because the northern branch instituted a standardized program of training for all its affiliated monasteries, while the southern patriarchs had little control over the training of their followers. (The lineage holders were recognized as carriers of the knowledge rather than as authoritative heads of an organization.) As a result, it is common for the patriarchs and teachers of southern Complete Reality Taoism to add "personal touches" to the tradition. Thus, by the time of its most famous fifth lineage carrier, Pai Yü-ch'an in the southern Sung dynasty (1127–1279), there were significant differences between what Chang Po-tuan had taught and what the followers of the southern branch believed and practiced.

Both the *Wu-hsüan p'ien* and the *T'ai-hsüan pao-tien* are texts from the late Sung, written after Pai Yü-ch'an's time. The teachings in the *Wu-hsüan p'ien* are similar to what Chang Po-tuan had taught. However, the *T'ai-hsüan pao-tien* recommends methods of cultivation of which Chang would have disapproved. These included using techniques of self-massage to circulate internal energy, ingesting herbs and fungi, swallowing the essence of the sun together with saliva, dancing the steps of Yü, and reciting special mantras. In fact, the methods of dancing the steps of power before going into the mountains to look for herbs and minerals, swallowing the essence of the sun, and projecting the spirit to appear as an apparition are all characteristic of the Shang Ch'ing school that flourished in southeast China between the fifth and tenth centuries, a form of Taoism that was rejected by the early southern Complete Reality practitioners. The *T'ai-hsüan pao-tien* is an example of the variation seen among the texts and teachings of the southern branch of Complete Reality Taoism.

The Outer Teachings: A Guide to Reading the *Tao-hsüan p'ien*

The *Tao-hsüan p'ien* is considered a text of outer teachings, and its contents can be understood easily by both initiates and non-initiates. Typically, the outer teachings of Taoism consist of the Taoist philosophy of nature and humanity, advice on spiritual daily living, and a brief introduction to the beginning stages of Taoist meditation. Practicing the outer teachings is often compared to walking on a wide, flat road. If you stray from the path, it is unlikely that you'll be injured. And should you stop to rest, it is easy to regain the ground you've lost.

The *Tao-hsüan p'ien* is closest to the *Tao-te-ching* in its subject matter. Like its famous predecessor, the text focuses on the Tao as manifested in the natural and social world and as practiced in statecraft and daily living. The Tao and virtue (*te*) are both integral to spiritual cultivation. In Complete Reality Taoism, cultivation begins with adopting a lifestyle conducive to clearing the mind and strengthening the body. Living a life of moderation, noninterference, quietude, and simplicity is the first step to building the foundation for the internal alchemical work necessary for attaining longevity and immortality.

The teachings of the *Tao-hsüan p'ien* are straightforward and easy to understand. You don't need to be initiated into the Complete Reality school or be supervised by a teacher to practice them. Such is the nature of outer teachings—they are accessible and safe.

The following are highlights of the teachings of the *Tao-hsüan p'ien*.

THE NATURE OF THE TAO

The Tao is the limitless origin of all things. There is a macrocosmic/microcosmic parallel between the Tao in nature and the Tao in humanity. This is because all things originate from the same source (the Tao) and follow the same principles. All things (plants, animals, humans, mountains, rivers, wind, and so on) are endowed with the vapor of the Tao, the life force of all creation. When the life force in us is plentiful and strong, we are healthy; when it is weak, we become ill; and when it is completely dissipated, we die.

THE TAO IN NATURE

When nature follows the way of the Tao, the seasons are timely and all living things are nourished and renewed. Because the internal universe of the body follows the same laws that govern nature, the body will be renewed when it functions according to the principles of the Tao. For the ordinary person, the vapor of life is used for procreation; for the Taoist adept, the vapor of life is preserved within and used to nourish and renew the body.

CULTIVATING MIND

A mind free of thoughts and desire is essential to realizing the Tao within. The empty mind is part of our original nature, and a primary goal of cultivating spirituality is to recover this original mind. The ordinary person cannot realize the original mind because it is blocked by the mundane mind of thoughts and desires. If these impermanent internal phenomena are eliminated, however, the original mind will emerge. Here we see the influence of Ch'an (Zen) Buddhism on the Complete Reality school. Ch'an taught that the true nature of mind is empty and that enlightenment is none other than recovering the true nature of the original mind. In the *Tao-hsüan p'ien*, the original mind is also equated with the celestial mind. This idea can be traced back to the *Tao-te-ching*: humankind follows the way of the earth, earth follows the way of heaven, and heaven follows the natural way of the Tao. For the practitioner of Complete Reality Taoism, to realize the empty mind is to merge with the celestial mind.

THE TAO IN THE SOCIAL WORLD

The principles of the Tao are also applicable to governing a country. Not all Taoist practitioners are hermits or monastics. Many choose to live as active citizens within society. The *Tao-hsüan p'ien*, like the *Tao-te-ching*, sees no conflict between public service and personal cultivation. This idea is embraced equally by both the northern and southern branches of Complete Reality Taoism. Throughout the centuries, many practitioners of both branches were active in government and community before retiring to devote their lives to Taoist cultivation. Some priests of the northern branch were even advisers to the imperial government and noble houses.

The *Tao-hsüan-p'ien* is one of the most accessible texts of Complete Reality Taoism. Its language is simple and its teachings easy to understand. Focusing on cultivating spiritual life, the text can be used as a guide for daily living for noninitiates, beginning practitioners, and adepts alike.

The Inner Teachings: A Guide to Reading the *Wu-hsüan p'ien*

The subject matter covered in the *Wu-hsüan p'ien* can be considered inner teachings, which are more esoteric and more difficult to understand than outer teachings. Typically, the inner teachings of Taoism consist of introductory information on the energetic structure of the human body and the methods of cultivating and circulating internal energy to attain health and longevity. Inner teachings traditionally are intended for initiates and are studied under the supervision of a teacher. While it is also possible for noninitiates to understand the inner teachings conceptually with the aid of a tutorial, using the text as an instruction manual in the absence of expert guidance is not recommended. The practice of inner teachings is likened to hiking a mountain trail. The path is narrow and rough, with many ups and downs. Resting places along this path are rare, and if you stray, you may suffer minor injuries.

The following are highlights of the teachings of the *Wu-hsüan p'ien*.

THE PRODUCTION AND CIRCULATION OF VAPOR AND FLUID

Vapor and fluid are the carriers of generative energy, and the production, preservation, cultivation, circulation, purification, and transmutation of generative energy form the foundation of Taoist internal alchemy. The production of vapor and fluid in the human body follows a biological clock.

THE COPULATION OF THE DRAGON AND THE TIGER

The dragon and tiger are respectively the yang and yin components of generative energy. Other names for the dragon are: the yang dragon that hides within the fluid, the yin within the yang (symbolized by the broken line flanked by two solid lines in the trigram *li* ☲), the vapor within the fluid, the vapor of pure yang, and the true fire. Other names for the tiger are: the yin tiger that hides within the vapor, the yang within the yin (symbolized by the solid line flanked by two broken lines in the trigram *k'an* ☵), the fluid within the vapor, the fluid of pure yin (or the vapor of pure yin), and the true water. The dragon and tiger are therefore *the* components or ingredients of mundane generative energy. Do not confuse them with their carriers, fluid and vapor.

Central to the preservation and cultivation of generative

energy is the process known as the copulation of the dragon and the tiger. The yin and yang components of generative energy meet and merge to become purified generative energy, which is also called the primordial vapor. The process begins with the vapors of pure yang (dragon) and pure yin (tiger) rising from the base of the spine and traveling separately up the spine and through the shoulder blades. When the vapors reach the head, they interact (copulate) and merge to become one unified vapor. This unified vapor descends to the palate of the mouth and is manifested as nectar, a sweet, sticky fluid. Swallowed down the throat, the nectar enters the middle *tan-t'ien* (in the area of the solar plexus) and eventually completes its circuit when it reaches the base of the spine again. (See figure 1.)

THE STAGES OF INTERNAL ALCHEMY

The internal alchemical work is divided into four stages: (1) transmuting generative energy (*ching*) into vital energy (*ch'i*); (2) transmuting vital energy into spirit (*shen*); (3) refining the spirit to return to the void; and (4) refining the void to merge with the Tao. (See figure 2.)

1. *Transmuting generative energy into vital energy.* The transmutation of generative energy into vital energy begins with the activation and production of the carriers of generative energy. The copulation of the dragon and tiger produces the primordial vapor, which is vital energy. The production and transmutation of generative energy occurs daily. Vapor, the carrier of the yang dragon, is produced around midnight. Fluid, the carrier of the

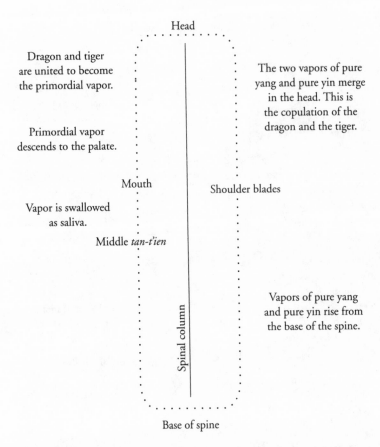

Fig. 1. The movement of the yang and yin vapors associated with the process of the copulation of the dragon and the tiger.

yin tiger, is produced in the morning. During the day, the carriers and the carried move to the places where the carriers are produced. Just before midnight, the two are transformed into the female and male components of generative energy. Around midnight, the cycle of production, circulation, and transformation begins again.

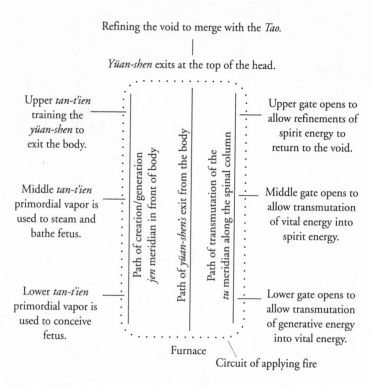

Refining the void to merge with the *Tao*.

Yüan-shen exits at the top of the head.

Upper *tan-t'ien* training the *yüan-shen* to exit the body.

Upper gate opens to allow refinements of spirit energy to return to the void.

Path of creation/generation *jen* meridian in front of body

Path of *yüan-shen's* exit from the body

Path of transmutation of the *tu* meridian along the spinal column

Middle *tan-t'ien* primordial vapor is used to steam and bathe fetus.

Middle gate opens to allow transmutation of vital energy into spirit energy.

Lower *tan-t'ien* primordial vapor is used to conceive fetus.

Lower gate opens to allow transmutation of generative energy into vital energy.

Furnace

Circuit of applying fire

Fig. 2. The internal alchemical process in the three gates and the three *tan-t'ien*s.

2. *Transmuting vital energy into spirit energy.* The transmutation of vital energy into spirit energy begins with the circulation of the primordial vapor. When fire (internal heat), fanned by breath, is applied to the primordial vapor, the vapor is driven to circulate inside the body. Initially, the vapor moves along the spine and the front of the body in a circuit called the microcosmic orbit. With time, the vapor will also move through the arms and legs in a circuit called the macrocosmic orbit. With each circulation, the primordial vapor is refined and transmuted into spirit energy. Spirit energy is also called the original or

primordial spirit (*yüan-shen*). The yüan-shen first manifests itself as a bundle of energy residing in the lower *tan-t'ien*. A practitioner who has reached this point of cultivation typically has a belly resembling that of a woman carrying a fetus; thus, the formation of the original/primordial spirit is referred to as the conception of the fetus in the womb. After the fetus is formed, it is bathed, nourished, and steamed continuously by the circulation of vital energy.

3. *Refining the spirit to return to the void.* When the fetus (the primordial spirit) is fully developed, it is ready to return to the void. At this time, the *yüan-shen* gradually rises from the lower to the middle and finally to the upper *tan-t'ien*. This stage of cultivation is referred to as "incubating the immortal fetus." The growth and maturation of the *yüan-shen* is likened to the development of a human fetus in the womb. Throughout this period, the immortal fetus is nourished as the practitioner gathers, refines, and circulates internal energy continuously. When the fetus is mature, it will exit the practitioner's body through the top of the head, appearing in multiple forms hovering around the corporeal shell. With time, the practitioner's body will radiate a golden aura, the skin will become bright and rosy, and the body will begin to resemble that of an infant.

4. *Refining the void to merge with the Tao.* The final stage of internal alchemy is to cultivate the void to merge with the Tao. In this stage, the *yüan-shen* is trained to return to the Tao, which is said to be its original home. The practitioner engages in the final stage of meditative stillness, called "nine years of facing the wall." At this time, the *yüan-shen* will travel farther

and farther from its bodily shell to learn the path of the return to the Tao. When the training of the *yüan-shen* is complete, it will make the final exit from the shell to merge with the Tao.

THE STAGES OF CULTIVATING THE MIND

The cultivation of the mind occupies an important part in Complete Reality training. The *Wu-hsüan p'ien* describes four stages of this cultivation.

The first stage involves quieting the mind. The goal is to minimize thinking, let go of desires, and get used to sitting in one posture for a period of time. You can think of it as relaxing the mind by not thinking and relaxing the body by not doing.

The second stage is called entering stillness. The goal is to continue to sit in stillness until there are no thoughts or desires. This stage is similar to Zen meditation.

The third stage is to use stillness to facilitate the movement of internal energy. When the mind is free of thoughts and desire and the body is still, internal energy can circulate and be refined. Thus, stillness is a precondition for the movement of energy. At this stage the microcosmic orbit is set in motion.

The fourth and final stage of cultivating the mind is to abide in absolute stillness. The goal is to cultivate the *yüan-shen* and train it to return to the Tao. Absolute stillness is synonymous with "nine years of facing the wall." In this stage, all movement stops: the *yüan-shen* leaves the body to learn to return to the Tao.

THE FIRING SCHEDULE

The firing schedule refers to the correct application of heat to transmute, refine, and circulate the internal energy. Correct amounts of heat applied at the appropriate time are necessary for the microcosmic and macrocosmic orbits to run properly. There are daily, monthly, seasonal, and yearly cycles of applying fire. In the *Tao-hsüan-p'ien*, only the daily cycle is described. Fire can be applied every day or over a number of days. It can be applied every hour each day, every two hours each day, or once a day for one or two hours. If fire is applied daily every hour, the alchemical process (which requires 360 circulations of the microcosmic orbit) can be completed in one year. It follows that if fire is applied once every day or once every few days, the alchemical process will take longer.

In the daily cycle, the fire travels through eight cavities in one hour. The eight cavities are represented as trigrams. The circuit and the locations of the trigrams in the body are shown in figure 3.

This description is meant to give readers enough background information to read the *Wu-hsüan p'ien*. Further discussion of Taoist internal alchemy can be found in my other books: *Harmonizing Yin and Yang* (Shambhala, 1997); *Cultivating the Energy of Life* (Shambhala, 1998); *The Tao of Health, Longevity, and Immortality* (Shambhala, 2000); and *The Shambhala Guide to Taoism* (Shambhala, 1996). Do not use the *Wu-hsüan p'ien* as an instruction manual unless you are under the tutelage of a teacher of the Complete Reality school.

The Secret Teachings: A Guide to Reading the *T'ai-hsüan pao-tien*

Secret teachings are the most esoteric and typically are available only to advanced initiates training under a teacher. The materials covered in the *T'ai-hsüan pao-tien* are considered secret

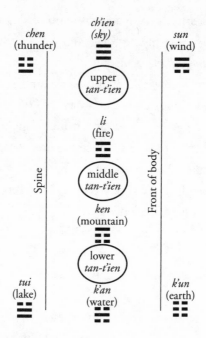

Fig. 3. The trigrams associated with the eight cavities matched to locations in the body.

teachings. They describe the internal energetic structure of the human body and outline the methods and techniques of cultivating and circulating internal energy for health, longevity, and immortality. While it is possible for noninitiates to understand the text intellectually with the help of a reader's guide, using the text as a training manual is not recommended without guidance from a qualified teacher of Complete Reality Taoism. The path of secret teachings is likened to climbing a cliff. Ascent is vertical; there are no resting places; and if you make a misstep, you could suffer serious injury.

The following are highlights of the teachings of the *T'ai-hsüan pao-tien*.

STRENGTHENING THE BONES, TENDONS, AND MUSCLES

The methods of strengthening bones, tendons, and muscles are unique to the *T'ai-hsüan pao-tien* and are the hallmark of the southern Complete Reality school. Practitioners of the southern branch often began cultivation after middle age, and these techniques were designed to strengthen older and weaker bodies and prepare them for the rigorous meditation practices.

For the practitioner beginning cultivation later in life, recovering tendon elasticity, spinal strength, and bone marrow density is important. A strong spine is necessary for maintaining the meditative posture to circulate vapor in the microcosmic and macrocosmic orbits. Older practitioners, especially householders, are more likely to have been married and had children, and they consequently would have less generative energy than those who begin their cultivation before puberty. Thus, it is recommended that these practitioners begin by regulating food, drink, and sexual activity and abstaining from excesses in daily living. Once generative energy is plentiful and the body is healthy, the practitioner can begin to gather and refine the primordial vapor.

THE PRODUCTION OF THE VAPOR OF LIFE

The process of the production of vapor in the body described in the *T'ai-hsüan pao-tien* is similar to that in the *Wu-hsüan p'ien*. The vapor of life is also referred to as the primordial vapor, the pure vapor, and the vapor of the void. If the primordial vapor is not used in procreation to conceive a human fetus, it can be gathered, purified, transmuted, and used to create the immortal fetus, or *yüan-shen*. Thus, cultivating health, longevity, and immortality all begin with the conservation of generative energy.

THE MICROCOSMIC ORBIT AND THE CIRCULATION OF FIRE

The microcosmic orbit and the circulation of fire is the key to the transmutation of generative energy to vital energy and vital energy into spirit energy. Breath is used to fan the internal fire necessary for the transmutation and to drive the vapor through the microcosmic orbit. The fire is referred to as the true fire or sacred fire. This fire is born in the "abyss of yin" and is the furnace or heat source for transmuting energies in the lower, middle, and upper *tan-t'iens*.

Two kinds of fire are circulated in the microcosmic orbit: the scholar fire and the warrior fire. The scholar fire is slow and warm and is used to incubate and bathe the fetus. The warrior fire is fast and hot and is used to drive vapor through the *tu* and *jen* meridians that make up the microcosmic orbit. Correct application of fire is necessary for the alchemical work to be effective. While it is not difficult to understand the theory of the circulation of fire, a teacher is needed to show the student when and how to implement the method.

The important points along the microcosmic orbit are shown in figure 4. This will be helpful for understanding the descriptions in the *Wu-hsüan p'ien* and the *T'ai-hsüan pao-tien*.

ACTIVATING AND CULTIVATING THE THREE *TAN-T'IEN*S

An important process in Taoist internal alchemy involves activating and cultivating the lower, middle, and upper *tan-t'iens*. The three *tan-t'iens* (elixir fields) are sometimes referred to as

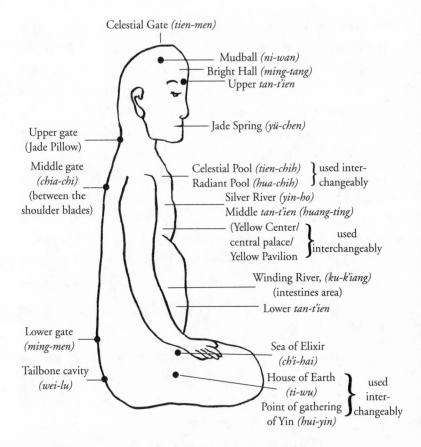

Celestial Gate *(tien-men)*

Mudball *(ni-wan)*
Bright Hall *(ming-tang)*
Upper *tan-t'ien*

Jade Spring *(yü-chen)*

Upper gate
(Jade Pillow)

Middle gate
(chia-chi)
(between the
shoulder blades)

Celestial Pool *(tien-chih)* } used inter-
Radiant Pool *(hua-chih)* } changeably
Silver River *(yin-ho)*
Middle *tan-t'ien (huang-ting)*
(Yellow Center/
central palace/ } used
Yellow Pavilion } interchangeably

Winding River, *(ku-k'iang)*
(intestines area)
Lower *tan-t'ien*

Lower gate
(ming-men)

Tailbone cavity
(wei-lu)

Sea of Elixir
(ch'i-hai)
House of Earth } used
(ti-wu) } inter-
Point of gathering } changeably
of Yin *(hui-yin)*

Fig. 4. The important points along the microcosmic orbit.

the lower, middle, and upper palaces. The *tan-t'ien*s are caul-
drons where the three energies—generative, vital, and spirit—
are transmuted. The lower *tan-t'ien* is activated when the lower
gate is open. Vapor from the lower *tan-t'ien* rises to the heart,
while fire from the heart sinks to the navel. This process is
called the "immersion of fire in water." The middle *tan-t'ien* is
activated when the middle gate is open. When this gate is open,

the practitioner must extinguish all thoughts and hold on to the undifferentiated primordial vapor (the One) in meditative stillness. The upper *tan-t'ien* is activated when the upper gate is open. When this gate is open, the Jade Essence (the primordial vapor) can be swallowed into the Radiant Pool (located approximately midway between the throat and the heart) and then routed down to the middle and the lower *tan-t'ien*s.

In the process of transmutation, vapor moves from the lower to the middle to the upper gates through the *tu* meridian along the spinal column. In the process of replenishing vital energy with spirit energy and replenishing generative energy with vital energy, vapor descends from the upper to the middle to the lower *tan-t'ien*s in the *jen* meridian along the front of the body.

FETAL BREATHING

The fetal breath is used to transport vapor through the body to nourish the internal organs. In fetal breathing, the breath is slow and deep, and there is no sensation of it rising or falling, or entering and exiting the nostrils. In the early stages of cultivation, when the carrier of generative energy is produced at the hour of *tzu*, fetal breathing can facilitate the movement of the vapor in the body. In the later stages of cultivation, fetal breathing is necessary for gathering the primordial vapor when it is produced.

LEAD AND MERCURY

Mercury is the yang dragon, the fluid embodied in the vapor. Its structure is described by the trigram *li*: the fluid is symbolized by the broken (yin) line embraced by its carrier (the vapor), which is symbolized by the two solid (yang) lines. This is what is meant by "the mercuric dragon hiding within the vapor."

Lead is the yin tiger, the vapor embodied in the fluid. Its structure is described by the trigram *k'an*: the vapor is symbolized by the solid (yang) line embraced by its carrier (the fluid), which is symbolized by the two broken (yin) lines. This is what is meant by "the lead tiger hiding within the fluid."

When lead and mercury are extracted from their carriers and are joined, the Golden Elixir, or pill of immortality, will be formed in the lower *tan-t'ien*. Lead will be transformed into the mysterious pearl, and mercury into the Yellow Splendor. These two purified essences of generative energy will merge to become the one undifferentiated primordial vapor. Health and longevity can be attained when the primordial vapor does not flow out of the body but is directed from the lower abdomen up to the head.

REFINING THE SPIRIT TO RETURN TO THE VOID

In this advanced stage of internal alchemy, the body of the practitioner emanates a golden light or aura, a sign that the barrier between the macrocosm of the universe and the microcosm of the body is dissolved. Now the practitioner can draw the energy of the Tao into the body and the *yüan-shen* can exit at will. While the spirit learns how to exit the body to return to its origin (the Tao), the light around the body is drawn inside to nourish the five viscera (heart, liver, spleen, lung, and kidneys). Until the *yüan-shen* is ready to make its final exit, the body must be kept strong, healthy, and nourished by the vapor of the Tao. If the cultivation of the body is neglected at this stage, the *yüan-shen* will weaken and may even "die."

DIFFERENCES BETWEEN FEMALE AND MALE CULTIVATION

The *T'ai-hsüan pao-tien* is one of the few internal alchemical texts that delineates different training methods for male and female practitioners. The text was written in the latter part of the Sung dynasty and shows the obvious influence of Sun Pu-erh (one of the first-generation Complete Reality students of Wang Ch'ung-yang), the founder of female internal alchemy.

The *T'ai-hsüan pao-tien* recommends that women and men follow different methods in the beginning and intermediate stages of cultivation. Because males and females have relative strengths and weaknesses due to gender differences in physiology and internal energetic structure, both must begin spiritual training by using their assets to strengthen their weaknesses.

The male practitioner must cultivate vapor and strengthen his generative energy by focusing on the kidneys, since energy from the kidneys is the source of *ching*. Once the generative energy no longer leaks out of the body, it can be channeled from the lower *tan-t'ien* into the *tu* meridian and routed up the spine to the Mudball cavity in the head. In males, blood is weak and vapor is strong; therefore the male practitioner must refine the vapor and use it to strengthen the blood. Also, because men are typically outwardly oriented, they must focus on stilling the mind and emptying desires. Once the male practitioner has cultivated receptivity and inner stillness, the generative energy will accumulate. With time, this energy can be transmuted and used to nourish the primordial spirit, or *yüan-shen*.

In contrast, the female practitioner must cultivate blood and strengthen her generative energy by focusing on the heart. To cultivate the primordial spirit, she must replenish the blood energy lost during her menstrual period by extinguishing the fire of desire. In females, blood is strong and vapor is weak; therefore, the female practitioner must refine the blood and use it to strengthen the vapor. Once the blood is strong, less energy will be lost during the menstrual period. With time, blood energy will strengthen the vapor, and vapor can be gathered in the breast and channeled to the kidneys, where it will rise to the Mudball cavity in the head.

Taken together, the *Tao-hsüan p'ien*, *Wu-hsüan p'ien*, and *T'ai-hsüan pao-tien* form an excellent introduction to the outer, inner, and secret teachings of Taoist spirituality. The *Tao-hsüan p'ien* can be used as a guide for daily spiritual living by initiates and noninitiates alike. For those who are considering initiation into a lineage-based tradition of internal alchemical Taoism or are simply curious about this form of Taoist practice, the *Wu-hsüan p'ien* and *T'ai-hsüan pao-tien* provide a glimpse of the deep teachings of Taoism.

Tao-hsüan p'ien

THE MYSTERIES OF THE TAO

1. The Tao

The Tao embodies the sky and the earth; therefore, it can give birth to them. Sky and earth embody the ten thousand myriad things; therefore they can nourish all creation. Despite their diversity, all things contain the spark of the Tao. The Tao is void and without form. When the Tao gives birth to things, however, structure and form emerge. Thus, form is the abode of the Tao, and spirit is its workings. All things follow the cycle of movement and stillness embodied in the Great Ultimate (*t'ai-chi*). Nothing departs from the principles the Tao.

2. The Mysterious Limit

That which is the Great Limitless (*wu-chi*) is called the Tao. That which is the Great Ultimate is called the body. Within the body is another body: this body is the celestial mind. When the celestial mind is anchored and still, it will keep the workings of the spirit in balance. Consequently, that which directs all things will be empty and numinous. When the spirit is numinous and clear, the ten thousand things will return to the Tao.

When the spirit is distracted by phenomena in the world, we will stray from our natural course. This is not because the Tao has distanced itself from humanity but because humanity has distanced itself from the Tao.

3. *Giving Life*

We are endowed with the energy of life when we are born. Accompanying the energy of life is original nature. Original nature is the spirit, and the energy of life is vapor. Spirit directs the body while vapor protects it. The spirit will not stray if we hold on to it; the vapor will not be lost if we nurture it. When spirit and vapor are one, the Tao within us will grow, and we will be able to attain longevity and be liberated from the dust of the mundane.

4. *Understanding the Principles*

The Tao does not owe its existence to anything; therefore it can give birth to all things. When manifested, however, the Tao is no longer empty. When its structure becomes function, the Tao gives birth to humanity. Because humankind has its foundation in the Tao, it can understand the constancy of the sky and the earth, discover the chambers of yin and yang, intuit the principles of procreation and transformation, and know its place in the grand scheme of things. The sage is someone who has penetrated these principles and understood the Tao.

5. *The Subtle Function*

Sky and earth are manifestations of yin and yang, and hidden in yin and yang are the secret workings of the universe. Yang initiates and yin receives. Yin gives form its substance and yang gives it essence. Ascending and descending, yin and yang are always together. It is in this way that all things are paired and grouped according to their kind. Male is associated with activity, and female is associated with stillness. Thus, looking at yin and yang, the nature of the sky and the earth can be intuited.

6. Humanity

When humans attain the vapor of life, they live. When things receive the vapor of life, they exist. The one undifferentiated spirit embodies both original nature and life, and original nature and life owe their existence to heaven. Some humans are kind and some are cruel. Some things are benevolent and some are malevolent. Why? This is because their vapors are manifested differently; it is not because they differ in original nature. Things may favor and emphasize different aspects of the Tao, but the Tao does not favor anything.

7. Embodying Form

Within the universe, there is nothing that does not follow some laws of existence, and there is nothing that does not embody the Tao. When things take on a form, they will develop tendencies. With the emergence of tendencies, the forms will have feelings. When feelings take hold, certain actions will follow. The Tao is manifested in forms. Thus, it can proliferate and be transformed. There is nothing that the Tao cannot become, and there is nothing with which it cannot merge. Although the dragon and the tiger are aroused, we must learn discipline and not be attached to their workings.

8. Dragon and Tiger

The dragon sighs and the tiger roars. The dragon embodies the principle of yang, and the tiger embodies the essence of yin. The yang dragon and yin tiger work in subtle ways. When the dragon sighs, clouds are formed. When the tiger roars, the winds whistle. When there are changes in the wind and clouds, thunder will shake the earth, and dragon and tiger will unite to become one breath. These processes are not driven by emotions. Rather, through the actions of the sage, the spirit moves in mysterious ways, allowing the ten thousand things to copulate and be created.

9. Leadership

Above, the sky covers; below, the earth holds. In this way, the ten thousand things are created and nourished. When a sage takes on the position of leadership, the nation will be peaceful and the people will be harmonious. Those with great abilities are given great responsibilities, and those with lesser abilities are given lesser responsibilities. The people are your brothers, sisters, and children. When you forget your desires, your people will be empty of desire; when you are content, your people will be content; and when you follow the principle of noninterference, your people will not interfere in the affairs of others. This was how Yao the sage ruled. Although he led his people for fifty years, he had no conception of what it means to rule and be ruled.

10. Virtue

In his position of leadership, the sage is not willful, egotistic, intellectualizing, or conceited. Rather, he is humble and considerate in his actions toward others. Because he is not willful, he can listen to his people. Because he is not egotistic, he can respect those who are virtuous. Because he does not intellectualize, he can understand the nature of things. Because he is not conceited, he can appreciate the achievements of others. Because he cultivates virtue and spreads it for the benefit of everyone, he is honored and respected by all.

11. Ruler and Ministers

A ruler cannot govern without ministers and advisers, and ministers cannot carry out their duties without leadership. If ruler and ministers work together, the nation will never be conquered. If the ruler treats her subjects as children, her subjects will regard her as their mother. When mother and son care for each other, there will be no gossip or slander. Just as the Tao gives life, a mother should protect the son and a son should care for his mother. If the mother and son within us are not separated, we will attain longevity and not die. The sage's desires are no different from those of others. It is only that there are no objects for the desires to attach themselves to.

12. The Tao and Virtue

The Tao is the greatest form of compassion, and virtue is the foundation of compassion. True compassion is not sentimental but follows the natural way of the Tao. True virtue is not righteous but also follows the natural way of the Tao. When you attain this virtue, you will attain the heart of the Tao, understand the principles, and penetrate the nature of the universe. When original nature is empty, you will value life and will come to know that all things are part of the Tao and virtue.

13. Succession

To name someone as successor, you must be sure that he or she is worthy. This is something the ancients had taught. The sage does not use his country to serve him; rather he works for the good of his nation. If the ruler can find a worthy successor, the people will be harmonious. Otherwise, the people will be rebellious. When King Yao retired, he named Shun as successor because he knew that Shun was virtuous while his own son was not. Shun named Yü as successor because he knew that Yü was worthy while his own son was not. Yü first named Yi as successor. Later he passed the kingship to his own son Kai because he heard the people sing praises to Kai and not to Yi. After that, kingship became hereditary. When a descendant is worthy, there is no need to look for a successor outside the family.

14. Protecting (the Body) and Keeping (the Principles)

Know the will of heaven and you will be able to preserve your body. Understand the words of the sages and you will be able to follow the principles of the Tao. If you can preserve your body, you will live long. If you live according to the principles of the Tao, you will be able to do great deeds. If you can be around for a long time, your family and country will not be endangered. If you can do great deeds, your children and grandchildren will always be safe. When there is no danger, you will never be harmed.

15. Emptiness and Clarity

If the mirror is empty and clear, you will naturally see the human mind's devious ways. If the mind is empty, you will naturally know the difference between good and bad. In emptiness form is exposed, and in clarity desire is revealed. Form and desire are both illusions and are not part of the underlying reality (of the Tao). Therefore, the great sages have always valued emptiness.

16. Preserving the Body

Where there is life, there will be death. Stray from the Tao, and you will lose your original nature. Just as horses without bridles run wild, people who do not know their original home are led astray by wayward emotions. If your desires are deep, you will bring ruin to yourself. Many people have destroyed themselves this way. The sage always follows the will of heaven. She understands her place in the grand scheme of things; she respects all things, preserves her energy, and cultivates her original nature. In this way, she can be at one with the ten thousand things.

17. Rituals and Music

Rituals and music cannot be absent in daily life. Ritual fosters respect in the heart, and music makes the body harmonious. If there is respect in the heart, everything will work properly. If the body is harmonious, the hundred guardian spirits will not stray from their places. When the guardian spirits stay within, energy will be plentiful and will flow into the Void.

18. Spirit and Breath

If you cultivate the spirit well, the light within will shine day and night. If you circulate the breath well, the void will be present in each cycle of inhalation and exhalation. The spirit resides in the breath, and the breath lives in the house of the spirit. When spirit and breath unite, you will attain great clarity.

19. Completeness and Brightness

If you focus solely on the inside, you will neglect the outside. If you focus entirely on the outside, you will neglect the inside. This is not the way of the Tao. What does it mean to be complete and bright? It means that there is no difference between the outside and the inside. Outside and inside exist only because form exists. When form is absent, function can be manifested. The way of the sage is circular; therefore he leaves no trace in the world.

20. Dissatisfaction

Those who are skilled are not satisfied; those who are unskilled are also not satisfied. The skilled are not satisfied because they are always ready to learn; the unskilled are not satisfied because they desire knowledge. If you think that your learning is inadequate, your nature will become bright. If you are greedy for knowledge, your nature will become dark and dim. If your mind is bright, you will enter the sacred. If your mind is dim, you will be trapped in ignorance. Enlightenment and ignorance are separated by a thin boundary. You should understand this well.

21. Learning

Anyone can learn. The intelligent person learns in order to understand the nature of things. The ignorant person learns in order to become an expert in one area. If you are knowledgeable in many things, you will not be anxious. If you can penetrate the principles of things, you will understand the whys and wherefores of things. If you are not anxious, you will understand the nature of all things. If you are connected to the origin, you will attain the ways of heaven and earth. This is because nature and heaven both follow the natural way.

22. *The Middle Way*

The sages follow the Middle Way. This is why they are more enlightened than the scholars, who are themselves more enlightened than the ignorant. The sage's learning is round, while the scholar's knowledge is angular. Knowledge that is round is adaptable, while knowledge that is angular is inflexible. This is why the sage's learning is higher than that of the scholar and the knowledge of the scholar is higher than that of the ignorant.

23. *Power and Respect*

The mind of the sage cannot be fathomed. When it is great, it can be transformed into the Limitless. When it is expansive, it can extend to all directions and surpass all things. Virtue is the driving force behind the three (realms) and the five (elements). Empty in the center, it anchors the four seasons and works for the welfare of all. Caring for all things, it has the capacity to understand the properties of the ten thousand things.

24. *Transformation*

The Tao in its greatness is the moving force behind the workings of the universe. Dark and mysterious, it is embodied in all things. Scrutinize it, and you cannot see its boundaries; try to tunnel into it, and you cannot reach its end. Expand it, and it can cover the earth and the sky; shrink it, and it can be contained in the smallest particle. It was there before we were born, and it has existed before things were named.

25. Penetrating the Subtleties

Just as a skillful tongue is the key to good speech and a strong hand is the key to a firm grip, attaining the highest principles is the key to penetrating the subtleties.

26. The Key to the Tao

The key to the Tao lies in the One Cavity. If generative energy is plentiful, vital energy will be preserved. If vital energy is preserved, the spirit will become omniscient. Do not deplete even one of these energies. If you lose one, you will lose the others. If you lose all the energies, how can you attain the Tao?

27. Gain and Loss

Do not be elated by gains or saddened over losses. If you are not satisfied with what you have, you will lose it. If you know what you have lost, you will be able to recover it. Those who possess much will lose what they have, and those who have lost what they have will regain what was lost. Only those who have attained the Tao will understand the true meaning of gain and loss.

28. Quieting the Mind

Plants grow because they are rooted in the earth. Humans live because the mind is rooted in original nature and life. When the soil is fertile, branches and leaves will be strong; when the mind is empty, the Tao and virtue will complement and strengthen each other. It is a pity that people do not know their original nature. They think that by desiring, they can capture material things in their minds, not knowing that it is their minds that are imprisoned. Using their feelings to hold on to things, they do not know that ultimately it is their feelings that are being controlled. Lose your attachment to things and you will gain. Allow yourself to be controlled by things and you will lose. Those who know the Tao understand this well.

29. Abandoning Intention

If you abandon intention, the birds will not be suspicious. If your intention is stirred, the birds will fly away. Why? This is because you can fool the form but not the spirit. Even if your spirit moves slightly, the other's spirit will know. This is the way things are: nothing can be hidden from the spirit. The sage knows that she and the ten thousand things are connected. Therefore, she always abandons her intention and keeps her mind empty.

30. True Emptiness

The Tao is invisible. If you try to grasp it, you will be imprisoned by appearances. The Tao is not empty. If you try to hold on to it, you will become attached to emptiness. Those who are attached either to appearances or emptiness do not understand the Tao. That which does not appear is true appearance. That which is not empty is true emptiness. True appearances and true emptiness are part of the ten thousand things. In function, they separate, and in transformation, they are inexhaustible.

31. *Having and Not Having*

To have and not to possess is the highest order of learning. To not have but to possess is the lowest order of learning. The wisdom of the sage is wide and deep; he knows that having does not mean possessing. The knowledge of the common person is narrow and shallow; he thinks that not having is not possessing. "I dare not put myself ahead of everyone"—these are the words of Lao-tzu. "I do not dare to think that I am righteous and virtuous"—these are the words of Confucius. "Having is really not having, and that which has substance can be empty"—these are the words of Yen-tzu. This is why those with great virtue occupy the highest places of honor and those of little virtue are the least worthy.

32. *Respect*

If you respect others, others will respect you. If you despise others, others will despise you. You should respect all things; above all, you should respect all people. The sage ruler considers his people his children. He honors those with abilities and values virtue. He does not belittle others; therefore others do not belittle him.

33. *The Art of Ruling*

There are five principles of ruling a country. Promote virtue in the nation and the people will be harmonious. Exercise integrity and the people will honor you. Teach the rites and rituals and people will respect you and each other. Use intelligence to observe the affairs of the country and the people will be prosperous and contented. Be honest and trustworthy and the people will support you. Although these principles have different names, they all come from the same source. The sage abides in emptiness and understands the nature of the Tao. Therefore, she can apply its principles with ease.

34. Observing the Tao

If you want to observe the Tao, observe the sea. Because the sea is the lowest point on earth, it can receive the waters of the hundred rivers and contain them. Great waves rise from its depths, and dragons, fishes, shrimps, and crabs frolic in its embrace. The mind of the sage is like the sea. It can contain the territories of the ten thousand nations. In cultivating the mind, the sage knows that the emptier the mind, the deeper it can penetrate the mysteries. In action, the sage knows that the more he gives, the more he will receive. Thus, nobles, ministers, and citizens all delight in his embrace. This is how the Tao is manifested in the world: it occupies the lowest place, but it is honored as the highest.

35. Emptiness

Form is created from emptiness. After form emerges, it seeks to return to emptiness. Mind and spirit are originally empty. Energy (*ch'i*), however, has form. If the mind is empty, the spirit will be calm and energy will be plentiful. If the mind is wayward, the spirit will leave and energy will be corrupted. The mind of the sage is always empty because she knows how to cultivate her spirit and energy.

36. *The Constant Mind*

If the mind is constant, it will dwell in the constancy of the Tao. If the mind is not constant, it will distance itself from the constancy of the Tao. If the mind is not corrupted, the constancy of the Tao will not change. If the mind strays, the constancy of the Tao will be unbalanced. The sages therefore always keep their minds clear and still and look inward into themselves.

37. *Dedication and Filial Piety*

Those who are dedicated are usually filial, and those who are filial are usually dedicated. When dedication is applied to the family, it becomes an offspring's filial gratitude to his parents. When dedication is applied to the nation, it becomes a minister's filial gratitude to the leader. A ruler is a parent; therefore, dedication to the leader is an expression of filial piety. Those who are dedicated and filial are simply following the principles of the Tao.

38. *Integrity*

Confucius would not drink water from a well belonging to bandits. Ts'ang-tzu turned his cart around in front of a village that had no sense of honor. The ancient sages refused to be acquainted with people with questionable attitudes. This is because they all followed the principles of the Way.

39. Moderation

Sages practice moderation. Attentive to the needs of humanity, they propagate the benevolence of the Tao. They do not favor one or the other but treat all as equal. They take from those who have and give to those who have not. Because of this, those who are disadvantaged will benefit, and those who are privileged will be humbled. The destitute will have enough; the rich will not be overly wealthy; and there will be harmony among all areas of society. This is because the sage follows the way of moderation.

40. Application and Function

If you seek the Tao in truth and honesty, the Tao will not stray from you. Apply the principles of the Tao at the appropriate time and you will receive its benefits. If the inside is stable, the spirit will be harmonious. If the outside functions smoothly, the spirit will be transformed naturally. If you observe the Tao in stillness, you will see that the Tao is not entirely without motion. If you observe the Tao in movement, you will see that the Tao is not entirely without stillness. This is because movement and stillness are both part of the Tao.

41. Spirit and Emptiness

The spirit embodies the Void of the sky and the earth. The movement of the spirit in things cannot be imagined, conceptualized, spoken of, or seen. Why? Because in thinking about it we will not understand it, and in conceptualizing it we will not be sincere. Moreover, that which can be talked about will not be pure, and that which can be seen is not real. The smallest can be the manifestation of the universe, and the largest can be hidden in a grain of dust. Entering water and not getting wet, walking through fire and not getting burned, penetrating metals and moving through stone, traveling to the realms of the living and the dead, and taming and commanding ghosts and spirits—these are some of the things that can be done by those who understand the Tao.

42. *Penetrating and Understanding*

Do not let the mind cling to things. Never force your actions in anything you do. If the mind clings, original nature will not emerge. If you force things, you will not penetrate the principles. Let your mind be united with the celestial mind and you will understand the workings of all things. Let your actions follow the natural way and you will penetrate the principles of all things. This is why the sages hide their minds within the natural phenomena and never force their actions.

43. *Fortune and Misfortune*

Those who follow the principles of heaven are favored by fortune. Those who serve themselves are visited by misfortune. If you follow the way of heaven, you will be content and want nothing. If you follow desires, you will never satisfy your wants. Those who are content are usually virtuous; thus, they are always protected by the Tao. Those who are greedy will lose everything. As they are blinded by evil ways, their attachment to material things will cause them to lose not only their original nature but also their lives.

44. *Knowing the Limits*

Fish swim in the deep rivers and wild beasts roam the mountains. Animals know their limits and do not go beyond their natural habitats. The human mind, however, does not know its original home and will often stray beyond its limits. The mind is the ruler of the body. Attain the (real) mind and you will live. Lose it and you will die.

45. *The Nature of Action*

When the Tao moves, the One gives rise to the two. In this way, creation emerges from copulation, good and bad oppose each other, life and death follow each other, hardness and softness conflict with each other, and gratitude and revenge balance each other. Those who do not understand the nature of action will fight the natural way. This is because they have been misled. However, those who understand the way of the Tao will preserve their form and let things exercise their natural functions. Knowing when to act and when to be still, they let their feelings return to their original nature, let their original nature return to emptiness, and let the emptiness merge with the ultimate reality. In this way, they are in harmony with the natural way.

46. *The Natural Way*

Spiders weave webs and dung beetles camouflage themselves as black balls—this is part of their nature. The sage learns by observing the natural order. He tells the people to hold on to simplicity, measure the amount of water in the well before they drink, and farm according to their needs. He does not encourage them to be scheming and knowledgeable. As a result, the people do not harm one another. Till the day of their death, they delight in harmony and simple happiness, never lodging complaints against each other. Although there are laws, there is no need to enforce them.

47. Natural Response

When deities appear, evil spirits will hide—this is the way of the Tao. When the dragon and tiger move, the weather will change. The sage tunes her actions according to changes in nature. This is what is meant by the mind responding naturally to the movement of the Tao. The ways of deities cannot be understood by evil spirits, and the activity of the dragon and tiger cannot be fathomed by animals and insects. Therefore, those whose actions can be predicted cannot be considered sages. Sages can do great deeds because their spirit is upright and they are steadfast in their courage. Because they teach according to the ways of the Tao, the world respects and follows them.

48. Pride

People who value their wealth tend to be proud. Those who value their political power tend to be willful. Those who value their learning tend to be haughty. Those who value being loved usually indulge in excesses. These are four illnesses that plague humanity. If you are proud, you won't last long. If you are willful, you won't survive. If you are haughty, you will achieve nothing. If you love yourself, you will meet with the misfortune of abandonment. Therefore, the sage is not proud when he is wealthy, not willful when he is in a position of power, not haughty when he is learned, and not egotistic when he is loved. He delights in simple living and does not expose himself to danger. In movement and stillness he is in harmony with the Tao and close to the natural way.

49. *Harmony*

When heaven loses harmony, the sun and moon will lose their light. When earth loses harmony, there will be landslides and avalanches. When a person loses harmony, the generative energy will dissipate. When the four seasons lose harmony, there will be disasters. Why? Because when there is harmony in heaven, the sky will be clear and expansive and the sun and moon will be bright. When there is harmony on earth, earth will be balanced and strong and the mountains and rocks will be stable. When there is harmony within a person, circulation will be smooth and energy will accumulate naturally. When there is harmony in the four seasons, changes in the weather will be orderly and the ten thousand things will be nourished. Those who follow the clockwise path are governed by changes in the yin and the yang. Those who take the reverse path, however, will be able to walk in the void.

50. *The Nature of Things*

Day and night are manifestations of the vapors of the sky; birth and death are manifestations of the coming and going of energy. The cycles of day and night and birth and death follow the principles of the nature of things. Where there is day, there is night; where there is birth, there will be death; where there is gathering, there will be dissipation—this is what we would expect normally. However, when the spirit is gathered, sky and earth will be bright and empty, and there will be no birth and death and no coming and going. You will arrive at your destination without having to walk there; things will come to fruition without planning; and goals will be accomplished without action. Understand these principles and you will be able to transcend life and death and be liberated from the confines of sky and earth.

51. Words and Speech

The sage uses words to reveal the Tao and speak about the intangible. The learned person uses words to describe the Tao and talk about the tangible. Words that are directed toward the intangible will reveal the principles of pre-creation. On the other hand, words that are directed toward the tangible will reveal the principles of post-creation. If the learned person can dissociate himself from form, abandon intelligence, gather and focus the spirit within, and not be attached to structure, he will become a sage.

52. Noncompetition

The Tao does not compete; those who compete do not follow the ways of the Tao. The Tao is not grasping; those who grasp do not understand the principles of the Tao. If you compete, you will attend only to differences in people's intelligence. If you grasp, you will always compare yourself with others. Concerned with petty matters, you will have abandoned the Tao and forgotten about virtue. The sage appears dull and dim, but her wisdom is like a piece of hidden jade. In her interaction with others she is not competitive or grasping. Because her spirit is in balance, she is in harmony with the sky and earth in all seasons.

53. *The Transformations of the Tao*

The Tao is transformed into vapor; vapor is transformed into blood; blood is transformed into form; form is transformed into things; and things are in turn transformed into other things. All transformations can be traced back to the One. Spirit is a manifestation of the One. When vapor is impure, the spirit will be evil; when vapor is pure, the spirit will be bright. Feelings can be transformed into nonfeelings, and nonfeelings can be transformed into feelings. This is because they both originate from the same vapor. Although things appear different, they all come from the same source. Observe the great transformation at the beginning of creation and you will understand the meaning of the formless and the nameless.

54. *Social Responsibility*

If you are a government official, you should apply the principles of the Tao to serve the people. If you are the ruler of the country, you should exercise virtue and serve the country. When the citizens are respectful and grateful to the government, it is a sign that the virtue of the ruler has reached the people. When there is freedom of speech, the feelings of the people will be communicated to those who rule. When no barriers exist between ruler and ruled, the country will be peaceful and prosperous. Those who use country and people to further their own interests, however, will meet with disaster.

55. *Honorable People*

Honorable people are clear about their intentions. If they choose to use their intelligence, they will serve the country; if not, they will live as a hermit in the mountains and forests. In positions of wealth and power, they are not proud; when impoverished they do not blame others. Advancing and retreating according to the situation, they balance movement and stillness. Following the will of heaven, they do not harbor deceit in their hearts. Such are the virtues of honorable people.

Wu-hsüan p'ien

UNDERSTANDING THE MYSTERIES

Humankind is born in the embrace of heaven and earth. Because our corporeal existence is dependent on the vapors of yin and yang, there is birth and death. Humans can be ghosts or immortals. Those filled with the vapor of pure yin are ghosts, and those filled with the vapor of pure yang are immortals. It is not difficult to use yin to refine yang or to use yang to refine yin. Throughout the ages, those who cultivate immortality have used yin to refine yang. When their yin disappeared completely, their yang became pure. When they were filled with pure yang, they became immortals. There are specific methods for refining yin and yang: for example, the numerics for stoking the fire must be correct, and the cycles of applying increasing and decreasing heat must be timely.

There is a cavity inside us called the Mysterious Female. If you understand the function of this cavity, the internal realms and the ten thousand things of creation will emerge within. This cavity is not a substantive thing, and to realize it, you must extinguish your thoughts, become unattached to forms, and hold on to the center. With time and practice, the Central Palace will be in a state of stillness. The vapor of yang within your body will grow naturally, and the vapor of yin will dissipate. This is what is meant by yang waxing and yin waning. I have received these ancient teachings from the enlightened ones, but I do not dare to disclose the secret workings of heaven casually. Thus, I have written down what I have learned in simple words, hoping that those who want to cultivate immortality will get a glimpse of the teachings. May we reach the shores of the immortal lands together.

The Tao cannot be described, although it is through words that we understand its teachings. The Tao is formless, but it is through form that we understand its principles. Once you have understood the structure of the Tao, you should forget about the words, just as once you have snared the rabbit, you should no longer think about the trap. Why? It is all the same principle: you need a raft to cross the river, but once you've reached the shore, you won't need it anymore.

Humanity receives the true vapor of the primordial yang. In the vapor are 384 golden pearls. Within each golden pearl are twenty-four smaller pearls, spread throughout the five viscera. This pattern parallels the 360 days of celestial movement. Yüan-ho-tzu said, "The workings of the human body and the universe follow the same principles." Shao Tzu said, "The foundations of the three realms are planted within us; everybody has a *ch'ien* (heaven) and a *k'un* (earth)." This is the way of things.

In the body, the two vapors in the kidneys begin their ascent at the hour of *tzu* (11 P.M.–1 A.M.). In the hour of *wu* (11 A.M.–1 P.M.) the vapors reach the heart. Interacting with each other, the vapors are routed to the liver and are steamed. At the same time, the fluid of the lungs enters the heart. The vapor of the

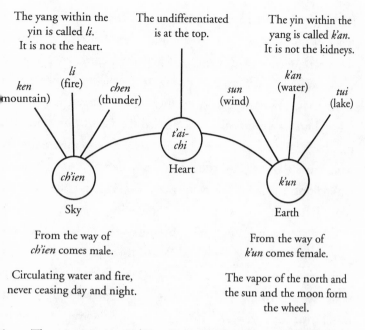

The yang within the
yin is called *li*.
It is not the heart.

The undifferentiated
is at the top.

The yin within the
yang is called *k'an*.
It is not the kidneys.

ken
(mountain)

li
(fire)

chen
(thunder)

sun
(wind)

k'an
(water)

tui
(lake)

*t'ai-
chi*

Heart

ch'ien

Sky

k'un

Earth

From the way of
ch'ien comes male.

From the way of
k'un comes female.

Circulating water and fire,
never ceasing day and night.

The vapor of the north and
the sun and the moon form
the wheel.

Fig. 5. The trigrams associated with the eight cavities in the circulation of fire (original illustration from the *Wu-hsüan p'ien*).

nd comfortable. Forget about forms and do not be attached) things in the world. Forget the mind and do not be attached) thoughts. When you hold on to the One within, you should e focused and not grasping. Be mindful, but at the same time t emptiness be your guide. With time, you will become adept quiet sitting and your thoughts will be still. When thoughts e still, yang will emerge. When the vapor of yang emerges, it ill rise and fall. The vapor rises from the base of the spine and cends to the area between the shoulder blades. Driven by the ind, it will rumble and roar and rise to the top of the head. he two vapors of yin and yang will interact and merge and

left kidney carries the fluid of the lungs and descends. The vapor of the right kidney, carrying the fluid of the liver, also descends. In the hour of *hai* (9 P.M.–11 P.M.), the vapors reach the kidneys. The fluid of the lungs enters the left kidney and is transformed into generative energy (*ching*), and the fluid of the liver enters the right kidney and is transformed into blood.

Primordial vapor dissipates with aging. When we age, generative energy and blood will wither, and death will come. The alchemical texts say, "When the five elements follow the forward cycle, you will be taken to the fire pit of hell; when the five elements follow the reverse cycle, the seven treasures will materialize on earth." Thus, the enlightened ones who cultivate immortality tell us that the dragon emerges from the fire and the tiger is born in the water. This is the principle of the reversal of the five elements. The path of reversal is equivalent to the path of the sacred, and the path of forward movement is equivalent to the path of the mundane.

If you want to attain immortality, you need to understand the wondrous workings of the three gates: in the first gate, generative energy (*ching*) is transmuted into vapor (*ch'i*); in the second gate, vapor is transmuted into spirit (*shen*); in the third gate, the spirit is returned to the void. Dissolution in the void is your goal. The techniques of the alchemical work in the three gates are transmitted orally. Bathe and steam for two months—this is the mystery of mysteries. The mnemonics can only be transmitted in detail from teacher to student. Therefore, I do not dare to speak about them casually. If you do not receive instructions from a true teacher, you will waste your time and effort and attain nothing.

1. The Emergence of Form

When the generative seed of the father is received by the procreative blood of the mother, a fetus is conceived in the womb. Within us is a spark of the primordial vapor, which is the foundation of creation and transformation. First to emerge in the fetus is the left kidney, followed by the right kidney. The kidneys give birth to the heart, the heart to the liver, the liver to the lungs, the lungs to the spleen, the spleen to the small intestines, and the small intestines to the large intestines. As the five elements transform each other, the bodily form emerges. After ten lunar months, the form of the fetus is complete and the child is born. Today, people know only how the body's form is created but not how vapor is transformed. They work only with the transformation of vapor and the transformation of form. They think that the area between the two kidneys is the place where creation takes place, and they say that the heart and the kidneys are fire and water, the liver and lungs are filled and hollow vessels respectively, and the spleen is associated with intention. This is all erroneous.

2. The Emergence of Vapor

After ten months in the mother's womb, the fetus will be filled completely with vapor. At conception, we receive the one spark of primordial vapor from our father and mother, which is channeled to the heart. When the vapor enters the heart, the heart is activated. With time, the one primordial vapor within the fetus will spread into the womb to nourish the unborn child.

Ghosts dwell in darkness, lost and confused and knowing nothing. They are like the drizzling rain enveloped in m fog and are untouched by light until they follow the spirit to enter the womb. When they come into with the light, they are no longer yin. In their encoun yang, they are transformed by the vapor. This vapor other than the primordial vapor called the Great Ultim mordial vapor rises and is separated into two vapors. A separation, the two vapors descend to the left and right embodying the two complementary opposites. Follow way of heaven, males are born. Following the way females are born. When heaven and earth interact, give birth to their six children. When these six move, transformed into the six meridians, which form a circ body. At this time, the body is fully equipped for gr transformation. Released into the world, the vapor comes a human.

If you study and practice the arts of immortality, value your body. Use the body to build a foundation help you to transcend the mundane and enter the case I have not described things clearly, I have inclu gram (figure 5) so that sincere students of the Tao c stand these teachings.

3. The Method of Quiet Sitting

Those who follow the ways of the Tao are not imp rules. When the body and mind are inclined, you s stillness. Close your eyes and mouth, sit upright, an and alert. You can cross your legs or sit in a positic

then descend to the palate in the mouth. When you taste sweetness, you should swallow the saliva and let it sink into the Central Palace. The classics of internal alchemy call this "blowing the winds of spring," or "blowing hard in the beginning and not feeling the breath at the end." If, however, you do not understand the principles of ascent and descent, the timeliness of applying fire during the day, the subtle functions of the three gates, and the mysteries of bathing and steaming, you will only waste your time and effort. No matter how much you practice, you will attain nothing.

The ancient texts say, "The immortals are unwilling to speak about the techniques of immortality openly because they are afraid that mortals in their arrogance would misunderstand the teachings and mislead others." Thus, people nowadays know only of earth immortals playing in the mortal realm and know little of what the spirit and celestial immortals practiced. The secret teachings of heaven are not taught casually. This is why I have refrained from describing the techniques in detail, letting the innermost teachings be transmitted orally, directly from teacher to student.

4. *Hyperactive Fire and Stagnant Water*

When fire is too active, it will rise without control. When water is stagnant, it will fall endlessly. If you use the correct method to regulate them and if the appropriate amounts are applied, the fire will not become aggressive and the water will not be stagnant. When stillness is attained naturally, the precious substance will emerge when it is needed and be dormant when it is not. The principles are encoded in mnemonics. If you do not have this knowledge, how can you transmute generative energy into vapor, transmute vapor into spirit, and refine the spirit to return to the void? Of those who study the Tao today, only a few have received the correct transmission of the teachings. This is because the principles are not revealed casually.

5. Bathing

Ten months in the womb and two months of bathing make up one year of 360 days. We will discuss the ten months of incubation in the womb later. Now, what is involved in the months of bathing? During the two months of bathing, fire is not stoked. Bathing can occur before, during, or after the ten months of pregnancy. The process is subtle; it is said that "it is applied and yet not applied." Those who study the teachings of the Tao must learn the method sincerely. The two months do not refer to the months of *mao* (fourth month) and *yu* (tenth month). As to how the fetus is liberated from the womb, these teachings are transmitted orally.

6. The One Cavity of the Mysterious Gate [also known as the "Mysterious Female"]

The cavity of the Mysterious Gate lies within. It is without structure and form and is limitless. Try to find it, and it will seem as if it is beyond thousands of mountains. Try to locate it in the heart, liver, spleen, lungs, or kidneys, and you will find nothing. Words cannot describe this cavity. If you try to grasp it, it is nowhere to be found.

7. The Medicines

Within the generative energy are vapor and blood, and within blood is generative essence. Generative energy and vapor both emerge with the Great Ultimate. The two interact during inhalation and exhalation. How can these substances be subjected to birth and death?

8. The Schedule of the Firing Process

When you stoke the fire, make sure that the fire travels one full cycle of circulation. You can circulate the fire every day for ten months or its equivalent of three hundred days or 3,600 two-hour periods. Or you can circulate the fire every hour, every two hours, or every day. Or you can select any hour during each two-hour period, or select any two-hour period during each day. The important thing is to do it naturally. If you do not know how to apply the fire, it will ascend and descend incorrectly. As a result, nothing will be accomplished. This is what the mnemonics say.

9. The Central Palace

Earth gives birth to the ten thousand things. The mind gives rise to the ten thousand thoughts. The mind is the earth and the earth is the mind. Therefore they are both called "the earth of the (celestial stem) *wu* and the (terrestrial branch) *ch'i* of the center." The center is the cavity of the Mysterious Gate. Extinguish the earth and all things will die. Extinguish the mind and all thoughts will cease. Many followers of the Tao look outside aimlessly for help. They do not know how to enter the center to look for the Tao.

10. Holding the One

To shed the shell, you must swallow the vapor into the belly. To become an immortal, you must stay in the mortal realm for nine years and perform eight hundred good deeds. While living in the earthly realm, you can travel to the sky, tunnel beneath the earth, and wander around the famous mountains and grottoes. Eight hundred days after you have completed the required number of good deeds, you will receive the golden writ and jade summons and will be listed in the roster of the immortals.

11. Liberating the Spirit and Shedding the Shell

Those who follow the Tao often do not understand the principles of stoking the fire, bathing, and transmutation. As for when and how to shed the bodily shell, these teachings are transmitted orally.

12. The One Cavity of the Mysterious Gate

The cavity of the Mysterious Gate is the most important gate in the body. This cavity is the mind within the mind. It is not made of flesh and blood, yet it is the spirit that directs everything in us. The spirit dwells inside a substantive form. It is there and yet not there. When ego is absent, the one cavity of the Mysterious Gate will emerge. However, even if there is only one small trace of ego present, the cavity will disappear. The sage Cheng Ho said, "When there is no perspective or opinion, the center emerges; when there are perspective and opinion, the center will not exist." The immortal of the Almond Tree said, "There is a secret working in the body—it is the mind free of dust." Everything about the cavity is described by these words.

The one cavity of the Mysterious Gate is the origin of all things. In movement, it interacts with everything; in stillness, it cultivates itself within. Existing and yet not existing, it is neither filled nor empty. Focus on it and it will become still. Moving without obstruction with the breath, it rises to the White Tiger at the left and emerges from the Green Dragon at the right. When joined, the two animals will rest in the area of the spine between the shoulder blades. When the spring wind blows, the furnace will be lit. When the fire is ignited, the vapor will surge up and penetrate the K'un-lun Mountains (the spinal column). Sky and earth will copulate and be united as one. When you feel the vapor descend to the palate of the mouth, you must swallow it into the Yellow Palace. Repeat this procedure three or four times a day. Focus on the lower gate for one hundred days, applying the technique of bathing for one month. Repeat this procedure focusing on the middle gate, and then for the upper gate. When the correct amount of fire has been applied, the spirit will emerge. When the spirit emerges, you must hold on to the One and nourish the child. After nine years of practice and eight hundred good deeds, you will rise to the sky in broad daylight. (See figure 6 on page 67.)

The Tao does not speak. Neither does it answer questions. Forget structure and form; look for the mercury and the lead within; and hold on to the one substance. If intention, body, and mind are still, the spirit will be clear and every inhalation and exhalation will be unobstructed. The six meridians will move toward original nature and original life, and the energies will return to the primordial source. When body and mind are in total stillness, the first yang will emerge and the second yang will follow. Heated by fire, the yang (vapor) will rise to the Silver River. The Jade Pillow and the Mudball cavities will be immersed in fire. Sky and earth will copulate and, joined together, will descend to the Bright Hall. When these processes occur, an aura of light will hover on top of the head like a bright mirror. As the vapor descends to the palate, the mouth will be filled with a sweet, fragrant nectar. Swallow this nectar into the Yellow Palace, and the body will radiate in golden splendor. The three parties (man, woman, and go-between) will meet, and the child will be conceived. When the first, second, and third sets of trigrams are firmly planted, you will enter a trance. This is the time for the spirit to leave the body and travel among the constellations and spin and whirl with the movement of the stars. In about a year, the cavity at the top of the head will open. This process is known as "transcending the mundane and entering the sacred." Continue to hold on to the One. After nine years, the alchemical work will be complete. With each step of progress, you will get closer and closer to the Great Cavern.

Today I have disclosed the secrets of the sages. Clean your ears, hold on to the spirit, and cultivate the stillness. Do not wait, or the lead will disappear and the mercury will dissipate. When it is time for you to shed the shell, you will know that you have not cultivated in vain. The secret teachings are transmitted only to those who are sincere. I hope that all who follow the Tao will complete their cultivation speedily.

13. The Medicines

When gathering the medicines, first collect the true vapor from the blood, then collect the true generative energy from the vapor. Blood and vapor are united when they reach the top of the head, where they are transmuted into fluid. When the true generative energy and true vapor flow to the top of the head, they are transmuted into the golden fluid. Flowing through the meridians, they become the white blood. The gold enters the Central Palace and is coagulated into the pill. When the alchemical work is complete, blood and vapor will become white blood and the true generative energy and true vapor will merge to become the pill. When the process of transmutation is complete, the spirit can exit and reenter the body naturally and freely. This is not a matter of imagination or visualization. Leaping to the top of the head, the spirit will travel beyond the confines of yin and yang. This is what is meant by "having a body beyond the body," and it is not as strange as it appears.

Notes for Beginning Practitioners

1. The Gate of the Mysterious Female

Dissolve the ten thousand things. Do not forget original nature but forget the act of forgetting. The wonder of wonders is not tied to a location. This is what the cavity of the Mysterious Gate is about. It is not the idle talk of using mud to craft a form.

2. *Penetrating the Gate*

When the gate of the cavity is pushed open, the two vapors will circulate in synchrony. When all is still within, the vapors will move naturally on their own, coming and going without notice. This is called turning the wheel.

3. *Breaking the Mirror*

When the mind is clear and original nature is anchored, the light will be gentle and bright as a polished mirror. However, if one thought arises, the mirror will break, and forms will arise. Those who cultivate the Tao must therefore not be attached. They must regard all appearances as originating from something other than their own original nature. This is why it is said, "The difficulty lies in the eyes; remember that beneath original nature there is no dust."

When thoughts arise, original nature will be shaken, and you will see ghostly images. If you maintain the stillness within, you will be able to respond naturally to these phenomena. If you are not attached to things, there will be no monsters.

4. *Fighting the Monsters*

When thoughts and desire arise, ghostly images and monstrous beings will appear and multiply. At this time, you must initiate the wheels of fire and water and send them through the three gates into the Inner Court. In this way, the Three Monsters (that block the gates) and the Six Thieves (of the senses) will be banished, and the ghostly images will disappear naturally.

When you feel the heavy weight of darkness descending, you should take the sword, walk the pattern of the Dipper, and send the wind into the furnace. Stoke the fires of the three yangs and sweep the evil vapors into the fire.

5. Setting Up the Foundation

Up to now, the work is similar to what the Buddhists call "compounding everything into one." The most important thing at this stage is to work steadily in the days and months ahead, training with discipline and diligence.

Those who understand the Tao, however, will realize that cultivation does not end here. The foundation must be built and the fires must circulate before the pill can be completed. When the foundation is stable and thoughts are extinguished, the light of the spirit will guard the body day and night. Your eyes will naturally see nothing desirable, and, in stillness, the one mind will hold on to the true mystery.

6. The Firing Schedule

The eight cavities form eight gates in the wheel of fire. The application of warmth, cool, cold, and heat must follow the principles of heaven and earth. The yin and yang fires of the four seasons must be timely. When all the procedures are followed correctly, the cinnabar grains in the cauldron will be transformed into the purple vapor.

Immortal Pai (Yü-ch'an) said, "The schedule of circulating the fire follows twelve periods. One period consists of five hours. There are eight regions in the body, and the microcosmic circulation completes one revolution in one hour. The alchemical work should be complete in one year." Those who understand these principles will gladly endure hunger and thirst to learn the methods.

7. Bathing

Bathing in the body means bathing in the vapors of the seasons. Bathing in the month means bathing and moistening the "head" of the pill. When Po-tuan talks about "the two months of the rabbit and the rooster," he is referring to the two months of bathing.

When generative energy is plentiful, when vapor is strong, and when the medicinal cauldron is warm, the "two and the eight" (that is sixteen, the age of male puberty) will arrive at your door and the roots will be firm. Draw (on *k'an*) to replenish (*li*), increasing the fire continuously. Clear the mind, extinguish the thoughts, and the Tao will endure.

When the vapor emerges, you must block the leakage. Lower the eyelids, gaze within, and extinguish all desires. Wait for the vapor to calm down, and then direct it to all areas in the body. If you do not have control over the vapor, the elixir will go to waste.

When you reach this stage, you must be aware of the danger of leakage. When the vapor is swirling within, you must preserve and cultivate it by closing the doors and abiding in nonaction.

The precious substance is fresh like the clear waters of a bubbling spring. It flows as slowly as the movement of ants and

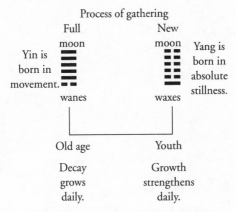

When lead meets *kuai*, the medicine is born;
you should gather it immediately.

When you collect the medicine,
pay attention to whether it is old or new.

When gold emerges, look far
and do not be tempted.

Fig. 6. The process of gathering energy. The waxing and waning of yin and yang (original illustration from the *Wu-hsüan p'ien*).

trickles out as thin as a strand of hair. When you feel the flow, you must close your eyes and focus within. The emptiness inside should feel filled yet empty at the same time. Be ready when the true vapor of the Palace of K'un sends heat shooting up the spine. Use the gentle wind of spring to fan the fire and lead it into the Celestial Palace (Upper *tan-t'ien*). Keep it locked within and do not let it leak out. After the vapor fills the head, let it descend. The earth element within should now be fertile enough to cultivate a forest of nectar.

In the human body, yang gathers in the head. The yin within the yang is called the true mercury. The five viscera are where

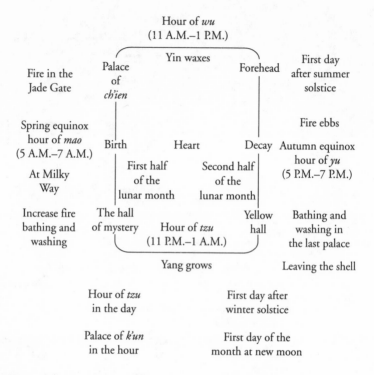

Fig. 7. The circulation of fire (original illustration from the
Wu-hsüan p'ien).

all the yin gathers. The yang within the yin is called the true
lead. Thus, the region above the heart is not purely yang and
the region below it is not purely yin. If you attain the center,
you will realize the director of all things. However, if you try to
look for it, you will find that it is invisible; if you try to listen
to it, you will find that it is inaudible. Only those who can tune
in to the internal universe will be able to resonate with it, and
only those who attain the center will be able to abide in true

stillness. If you can attain the center that is always still and practice the methods until you are competent, you will be able to penetrate the secret workings of the sky and the earth and all things. (See figure 7.)

T'ai-hsüan pao-tien

THE SACRED TREATISE

ON THE GREAT MYSTERY

Part One

1. The Numinous Spirit and the Celestial Phenomena

The energy of the void gives birth to spirit; the spirit of the void gives birth to transformation; transformation in the void gives birth to phenomena. All things originate in the primal void. The primal void is present in the sky and the earth; it is not tied to directions or location, and it is neither energy nor form. Manifested as phenomena, that which is clear becomes sky, and that which is muddy becomes earth. After the clear and the muddy have separated, humanity is born. Thus, humankind possesses both the clear and the muddy. Even after the clear and the muddy are separated, the primal void is still embodied in them. Purify, temper, and hold on to the primal One, and the white in the void will emerge. When the white in the void emerges, that which is muddy will become clear, just as when the mind is empty, the spirit will be naturally bright. The workings of heaven will be known to you; ghosts and spirits will be yours to command; and the mysterious workings of yin and yang and the ten thousand things will be yours to understand. The way of immortality, therefore, lies in cultivating the void in the spirit and in separating the clear from the muddy.

2. *The Vapor of the Void Resonates in the Cavern*

Vapor is the master of phenomena and can be clear or muddy. The clear makes things rise and the muddy makes things take root. If there is no muddiness, form cannot exist. If there is no clarity, enlightenment is not possible. If you can attain clarity, the true yang will be empty, and you can merge with all things. Departing from death and entering life, you can change your form and transform your body. When energy is merged with the void, the spirit will become numinous. If you want to attain the numinous spirit, you must first empty your mind and cultivate the vital energy (*ch'i*). Extinguish your thoughts, focus the spirit, and conserve your vital energy. When vitality is conserved, it will become numinous and will resonate with all things. The sacred transformation follows the subtle ways of the sky and the earth. If you succeed in cultivating vital energy, you will attain the spirit of the cavern, and eventually you will be able to resonate with things in all directions. This is called following the principle of ceaseless circulation.

3. *Strengthening Generative Energy to Preserve Life*

Generative energy (*ching*) is the true essence. The true essence is the true beginning of all things, the origin of yin and yang, and the root of both life and death. If you want to preserve life, you must strengthen generative energy. Generative energy is the key to cultivating vital energy and nourishing spirit energy (*shen*). When vital energy is stable it will become thick and heavy. The secret to strengthening generative energy lies in the technique of attaining the primal. When spirit is still, life energy will be preserved. Vapor is the foundation of life. The enlightened ones of past and present cultivated vital energy and strengthened generative energy in order to preserve life and attain longevity. Those who are familiar with the methods will know that they must first prevent generative energy from dissipating. Otherwise, vital energy cannot be cultivated. When generative energy is stable, apply fire to circulate it. With time, generative energy will be strong. Next, use the breath to move vital energy around while continuing to cultivate generative energy. Once these processes are complete, the mysterious fetus will be formed. Preventing generative energy from dissipating and circulating vital energy without ceasing—these are the keys to attaining the subtle and the mysterious.

4. *The Copulation of Sky and Earth*

Sky gives birth to vapor, and earth gives birth to form. Vapor is the master of life, and blood is the root of form. Those who understand the principles of heaven will know how to cultivate life, and those who understand the principles of earth will know how to cultivate vapor. The enlightened ones tell us that vapor rises upward from the (lower) elixir field (*tan-t'ien*). If you don't want this vapor to dissipate, you must direct it to move from the right kidney through the abdomen and down to the leg.

From the foot, let it ascend the right side of the body into the right arm. Then, move it up to the shoulder blade and bring it into the ears and the brain. From there, let the vapor descend into the left ear, down through the shoulder blade, and into the left arm. Then, direct the vapor down the left side of the body, letting it run through the abdomen and down into the left leg. Finally, let the vapor rise from the foot to return to the (lower) elixir field. At midnight, quiet your mind and still your breath. When the vapor rises to the gate at the top of the head, a cold vapor will penetrate the Radiant Pool. When you hear the sound of running water, this is a sign that the primordial vapor is born. The primordial vapor moves naturally in the sky and the earth, penetrating all the circulatory channels in the body. When you feel it moving in the left side, you should use the right hand to massage the left side of the body; when you feel it moving in the right side, you should use the left hand to massage the right side of the body. When the vapor of life flows ceaselessly, sky and earth will copulate, and the internal universe will mirror the external universe. Practice these techniques diligently, and with time you will obtain results. After directing the vapor through its complete circuit three thousand times, the primordial vapor will circulate on its own. Your body will become like that of an infant, and you will neither grow old nor die.

5. The Creative Power of Yin and Yang

The male follows the principles of the sky. Receiving the vapor of yang, the kidneys are first to emerge. The female follows the principles of the earth. Receiving the vapor of yin, the blood and the heart are first to emerge. Therefore, to attain immortality, the male must cultivate vapor and conserve generative energy, and the female must cultivate blood and preserve the spirit. Because they follow different principles of creation, female and male must use different techniques of cultivation. The male must focus on the kidneys and strengthen the generative energy to cultivate vapor. In this way, the energy can be channeled from the lower abdomen up the spine and into the Mudball cavity. This process is known as returning to the primal state. The female must focus on the heart and cultivate the spirit so that the fire is not aroused. She must channel the vapor stored in the breast into the kidneys, and then let it rise to the Mudball cavity. This process is called transmutation into the realized being. If these procedures are practiced correctly for one hundred days, the generative energy of the male will not leak out. His body will become like that of an infant, and the spirit will be numinous. For the female, her blood will not be aroused, her spirit will be still, and she will return to virginity. Her vapor in the two meridians will be tamed, one transmuted into breast energy and the other transmuted into blood. This method is subtle beyond imagination. With time, black hair will grow long and healthy, the breasts will flatten and become firm, the position of the kidneys will change, and her body will become like that of an infant.

6. Natural Fetal Breathing

If you want to circulate vapor, you must first breathe quietly like a fetus. Fetal breathing is the natural way of breathing. The breath must be regular, and there should be a set number of breaths in a given period of time. The breath also must not rise or fall, nor exit and enter through the nostrils, but move around internally. You should practice fetal breathing at midnight, when the vapor is born. After one hundred days, you should be able to conserve vapor by slowing the breath. First, get the vapor to penetrate the ears. Then, cover the ears with your hands. At midnight, use the breath to move the vapor around. With time, the passage to the ears will be open. Once the passages to the ears are opened, the breath will not pass through the mouth and the nostrils, and you will be able to stop the breath. When vapor starts to circulate, you can cultivate and gather the vapor at midnight. When the primal vapor moves, cover the ears with your hands and allow the vapor to rise. Then massage to direct the vapor to move counterclockwise until it flows back and forth between the skin and the internal organs.

7. Lead and Mercury Germinate

The south gives birth to fire, and fire gives birth to the heart. The heart is the cinnabar grains, and within the cinnabar grains is mercury weighing four ounces. The north gives birth to water, and water gives birth to the kidneys. The kidneys are green metal, and green metal gives birth to lead, also weighing four ounces. Mercury emerges when the heart is quiet, and lead emerges when the kidneys are not aroused. Lead and mercury rise and fall, meeting in the golden cauldron where they are transmuted into the Great Pill and crystallized into the ultimate medicine. If the heart is not still, mercury will not appear; if you lose softness, the cinnabar grains will wither. When the cinnabar grains wither, the face will lose its shininess and appear pallid, and the skin will lose its brightness. If the kidneys are aroused, lead will not appear. If you lose the lead, the green metal will wither. When the green metal withers, the face will lose its luster and appear dark, and the skin will become dry and brittle. Why? This is because the vapors of lead and mercury have lost their roots. Lead and mercury will not grow if you have not received the teachings from enlightened teachers. They also will not grow if you practice the methods incorrectly. Therefore, the immortals cultivate vapor to preserve the kidneys and allow the lead to grow by stilling the spirit and clearing the mind. Because they know how to let mercury and lead mutually create each other, they can stay healthy in this realm for a long time. Everything hinges on understanding the origin of the two vapors (of lead and mercury). Therefore, clear the dust out of your ears before you listen to these teachings.

SECTION TWO: THE METHODS OF CULTIVATING THE ULTIMATE REALITY TO MERGE WITH THE SACRED

1. Spirit Transmuting Spirit

Use the void as structure, and use the light of stillness as function. Yin and yang cannot be confined to a numerical scheme, and sky and earth are not reducible to "things." As for humanity, it is too attached to the dust of the world to understand these principles. From ancient times, the methods have not been spoken of casually; therefore not many people have attained longevity and immortality. Only the enlightened ones returned to simplicity and purity, cultivated clarity and brilliance, and used stillness to hold on to the underlying reality. The key lies in extinguishing wayward thoughts from the ordinary mind. Realize the true spirit, and the void will naturally emerge. Merge with the formless, and you will be able to wander in the three realms of the subtle cavern, penetrate the roots of life and death, and arrive at the ultimate answer to gain and loss. This process is known as the spirit resonating. There is nothing that the spirit cannot do. When spirit transforms spirit, the spirit will always be within you. The spirit within is the same as the true spirit of the sky and the earth and of all phenomena. The transformation of the spirit lies in abiding in stillness. When mind and body are still, the true vapor will rise. When you feel the true vapor rising, put the left hand on top of the right hand. Then, touch the top of the head with the right hand. After three thousand sessions of practice, the spirit will exit the body.

2. *Vapor Transmuting Vapor*

In order for the vapor to become numinous, we need to practice inward gazing, apply the technique of massage, and realize the natural sacred numerics (the internal dimensions of the cauldron) within. When vapor is numinous, it will naturally follow and move with intention. If the mind is wayward, however, vapor will dissipate. If you are anxious, worried, elated, or excited, the vapor will be unstable and lose its original essence. Therefore, the enlightened ones know that to cultivate vapor, they must first get rid of all attachments in the mind. The movement of the vapor begins at the (lower) elixir field. First, it circulates within the musculoskeletal shell. Then it visits the three palaces and lingers there. Exiting the palaces, it can move rapidly or slowly. Carried by the three carts, it will move up to the Mudball cavity. I will not dwell too much on the secret teachings here. It is sufficient to know that if you want the vapor to be strong, you must be disciplined in your practice. You can use a partner to help you to circulate the vapor. You can also direct the vapor from the waist to the top of the head by massaging yourself. When you feel the vapor moving up, swallow the nectar of the Radiant Pool (*hua-chih*) forty-nine times. The true vapor will then become stable and strong. With time, it will be transmuted into the original primal vapor. This is what is known as using vapor to transmute vapor to attain immortality.

3. Generative Essence Transmuting Generative Essence

The aim of preserving generative energy is to refine vital energy. When vital energy is strong, generative energy will also be strong. When generative energy is secure, it can be refined. Today, people know only how to refine vital energy; they do not know how to refine the true generative essence. They also do not know that the enlightened ones refined their generative energy by preserving and securing it. It is only when generative energy does not dissipate that it is possible to arouse its movement and refine it in earnest. To preserve the generative energy, you must lock the nine gates and sit quietly to secure it within. Generative energy begins its movement from the base of the spine. After it is awakened, for three hours vapor and generative energy will interact nine times in the area below the navel. When you feel the arousal of generative energy, you should apply the technique of refinement during the hours of *tzu* (11 P.M.–1 A.M.) and *wu* (11 A.M.–1 P.M.). Circulate the vapor 360 times during these two periods, and in ten days the true generative essence will emerge naturally. It is important that you absorb the energy resulting from the copulation of yin and yang. In this way, the true generative energy will return to its vapor form to nourish your body. Remember to clasp your hands together with the thumbs locked around each other. When all is still, let the vapor surge upward. Even when generative energy is aroused and moving, it will no longer leak out of the body.

4. Relocating Heaven and Earth

Males receive more of the pure yang of the sky, and females receive more of the pure yin of the earth. The path of pure yang is easier to attain than the path of pure yin. Therefore, in order to help women and men refine their vapors of life, the enlightened ones have come up with the methods of "transforming the female into the male" and "transforming the male into the female." In women, blood is strong but vapor is weak. Therefore, female practitioners must refine the blood and strengthen the vapor. In men, blood is weak but vapor is strong. Therefore, male practitioners must refine the vapor and strengthen the blood. Women and men both partake of the true energy of the sky and the earth. Therefore they are capable of relocating the sky and the earth inside their bodies. To refine the primal vapor and still the spirit, men must first focus on the mind, hold on to its oneness, and not let a single thought or desire arise. For the male practitioner, the methods all come down to accumulating generative energy and nourishing the spirit. Women, on the other hand, must refine the blood and pull the energy in from the breasts. To facilitate this process, they can massage the face with their hands. If the female practitioner cannot get the vapor to circulate in a counterclockwise direction, the transmutation will not occur.

5. Holding Yin and Yang in Your Hands

The left hand is yang; internally, it is connected to the kidneys. During the hour of *tzu* (11 P.M.–1 A.M.), vapor emerges from the kidneys, and spirit is born in the heart. At this time, form a fist with the left hand, close the left eye, and focus on the kidneys. Let the vapor move up to the left eye and then down to the left hand. Open the hand and open the eye after 360 circulations. In the hour of *wu* (11 A.M.–1 P.M.) the vapor will descend from the heart and the spirit will ascend from the kidneys. At this time, form a fist with your right hand, close the right eye, and focus on the heart. Let the vapor move up to the right eye and then down to the right hand. Open the hand and open the eye after 360 circulations. Practice this for three thousand days and you will have knowledge of events tens of thousands of miles away. You will see all the phenomena in the sky, earth, mountains, rivers, stars, and planets. Your spirit will become numinous, and you will understand things that the typical person cannot even begin to comprehend.

6. Fetal Inhalation and Exhalation

First, regulate the breath until there are no signs of inhalation and exhalation. Lock the vapor within and move it to the Radiant Pool cavity. After three thousand sessions of practice, the true generative essence will be strong. After fetal breathing has started, the saliva will be transformed into the mysterious pearl and can be regurgitated or swallowed back in. With time, the Tailbone (*wei-lu*) cavity will be locked and secure. After the true generative essence has emerged and the fetal breathing has become regular, the mysterious pearl will be formed. When the pearl can move from below up to the Mudball cavity without obstruction, you will attain longevity.

7. Lead and Mercury Become Precious Substances

The true generative essence gives birth to lead, and lead gives birth to the Yellow Splendor. When the spirit is still, mercury will emerge. Mercury gives birth to the mysterious pearl because it is the vessel holding the moisture. When mercury emerges, the vapor will be able to rise and fall and swirl and tumble. With time, the saliva will become a thick nectar and will drip down the throat to enter the Yellow Palace. During this time, more liquid will materialize on your tongue. The lead follows the movement of the breath and gives birth to the Yellow Splendor. The emergence of lead will prevent the breath from going up or down, allowing it to circulate left and right instead. With time, the breath in the abdomen will become still. Urinary secretions will take on a tint of green. Now the breath can move in and out naturally. If the vapor wants to move, it will penetrate the Tailbone cavity and come out as a liquid with a golden tint. This is what the enlightened ones mean by refining the lead and mercury and transforming them into the precious substance.

SECTION THREE: THE METHODS OF CULTIVATING THE UNDERLYING REALITY TO ATTAIN THE WONDROUS

1. *Spirit Emerging from Spirit*

Spirit can emerge from form when spirit energy is refined. What do we mean by refining spirit energy? It is none other than centering the mind. When mind is centered, the spirit will become still. If you don't want to grow old and senile, your spirit must transcend this life. To let the spirit emerge and transcend mortality, the spirit must be realized completely. Many books on the arts of immortality talk about preserving the underlying reality but neglect to mention realizing the spirit and refining it. To cultivate the spirit and refine the underlying reality, the mind must be like the bright moon. When the underlying reality is refined, it must first rise to the Mudball cavity and then fall into the sea of the elixir. With practice, a halo of light will hover around the body. When the light emerges, many forms will emanate from the body. This is the natural outcome of cultivating the spirit. Because the spirit exiting the body is born from the spirit within, this process is called spirit emerging from the spirit.

2. *Vapor Stabilizing Vapor*

The true vapor preserves the underlying reality within. Refine the vapor, and the years of your life will be like that of the sky and the earth. Vapor is entwined in the root of the Tao, for the

Tao is born of vapor. Vapor permeates space, and if the true vapor is not stirred, you will attain longevity. Vapor moves and circulates in the body. To refine it, you must know that it emerges from the lower elixir field at midnight. When you sense its emergence, you must move it from the place where it is born and direct it into the heart. When vapor is aroused, massage your body strongly with your hands to help it circulate. With continued practice, your complexion will be bright and rosy. The vapor will be pure and will not dissipate. Eventually, you will attain immortality.

3. *Preserving Generative, Vital, and Spirit Energies*

Those who cultivate the Tao must preserve the generative, vital, and spirit energies. When generative energy is strong, the skin will be bright and shiny and the sense of hearing will be enhanced. When spirit energy is strong, the face will be rosy and the eyes clear. When vital energy is strong, the voice will be strong and the body will feel light. Those who cultivate must aim to be filled with all three energies. Only then can you still the mind and attain the empty grotto within. Only then can the vapor move up and down without stopping. To strengthen the generative essence so that it can return to its primal form and not be dissipated, you must first still the mind. Swallow the thick nectar forty-nine times. Let the spirit reside contentedly within. Let the mind be as clear as the bright moon shining on the body. Let the vapor move strongly up to the Mudball cavity. Accumulate generative energy, do not let it leak out, and move it upward together with the vapor. If you practice these techniques diligently, the nine cavities will be bright and clear, the four limbs will be strong and healthy, and you will attain longevity.

4. *Extinguishing the Forms*

Forms originate from the vapors of the sky and the earth. Our goal in the mortal realm is to get rid of desire and attachments so that when we die we can shed the bodily shell and liberate the spirit from the dust of the world. Thus, in life, our goal is to extinguish the forms and turn them into shadows. In death, our goal is to focus the spirit and send it into the realm of the underlying reality of the Tao. The methods are defined very clearly. After the forms dissolve, you should walk toward the sun at sunrise on the winter solstice and climb up a mountain. If you hold a red mushroom in your hand and stand under a large pine tree, ghostly figures will appear and walk toward you. Call on the Celestial Wolf seven times, and the apparitions will turn around and vanish into a black fog. After this, the yin within you will be purged completely, and the ghostly shadows will no longer attack you. At the time of death, gather the spirit. The enlightened ones said: When spirit does not dissipate, generative essence will not dissipate.

5. *Banishing the Soul*

The soul is particular to the human. When it is bright and virtuous, it is the spirit. When it is attached to desire and evil, it becomes a monstrous shade. Those who cultivate the Tao must banish the monstrous soul and allow the spirit to emerge.

When the light of the spirit is projected out of the body, extraordinary beings will appear, either to welcome you to the immortal realm or to stop you from entering. Make sure you obey their orders.

6. *Transforming Old Age into Youth*

When you are old, you are weak; when you are young, you are strong. This is usually how it is. It is possible, however, for the old to be stronger than the young. This happens when the older person does not waste the primordial vapor and the young one dissipates the generative essence. The enlightened ones have designed methods to allow the old to return to their youth by strengthening their vapor. If you want to regain your strength and vigor, you will need to ingest the primal elixir of the nine immortals. Follow the correct procedures of refining the vapor and stilling the spirit. Fill the body with the eighty-one drops of the true elixir. At first the nectar will not feel sweet, but with time it should. When you have returned to the body of a youth, you should massage to direct the vapor from the heart to the kidneys. Within seven days, your body will become like that of an infant.

7. *Attaining Longevity*

Longevity can mean lengthening your life and not dying. It can also mean that when you shed your shell, your spirit does not die with the body. If you want to attain longevity in the earthly realm, you must refine yourself. Turn toward life before your bodily shell has run its course. One way to lengthen your life span is to find the right medicines and ingest them. Examples of such medicines are evergreen needles, pine cones, and the three yellows of the earth: the yellow earth, the yellow essence, and the essence of chrysanthemum. It is also possible to cultivate the great void by stilling the spirit. If you choose the latter path, you must focus on the kidneys and refine the vapor.

Part Two
SECTION ONE: THE METHODS OF REFINING THE MUNDANE AND TRANSFORMING IT INTO THE UNDERLYING REALITY

1. The Bones Become Weightless

Bones are made from the distilled vapor of yin and yang and are formed in the womb. Receiving the primordial vapor, they grow from young to strong to old. Within the bone is the marrow. Transformed into generative essence, the marrow becomes the primal root of the body, penetrating the tendons and meridians. The kinetics of body movement are built on the moisturizing properties of this vapor. When vapor and blood are plentiful and strong, the bones will feel light. Bones receive moisture and nourishment from blood. Thus, limb movement is affected by the amount of blood and marrow in the bones. When vapor and blood are weak, the bones will feel heavy. As a result, marrow will wither, generative essence will disappear, and we will die. The enlightened ones begin their cultivation by refining the blood and transmuting it into vapor. When the vapor begins to circulate, they work on refining the bones. Later, when the spirit is numinous, they refine the mind until there are no attachments. When vapor is like spring water, it is time to start the process of steaming. The generative essence is bathed in moisture and circulated together with the blood. When generative essence is transmuted into white jade, you will be well on your way toward immortality.

2. *Refining the Vapor and Completing the Cultivation of Stillness*

Vapor emerges according to cycles of time, and its properties are determined by form and governed by principles. At midnight, when the primordial vapor is born, you will hear a rattling sound, as if wind and rain are beating on your eardrums. When the vapor reaches the height of its flow, the sounds will resemble a ringing bell. In the daily cycle, the vapor emerges in the middle of the hour of *tzu* (II P.M.–I A.M.). If you are a seasoned practitioner, you will see the lights of the stars when you close your eyes and turn your attention upward, for these are signs that the vapor is rising. After the vapor has risen to the top of the head, it will circulate downward, tumbling and swirling toward the tailbone. From there, the vapor will move up again through the area between the shoulder blades to enter the Mudball cavity. From the Mudball cavity, it will descend to penetrate the nine cavities in the head. Moving through the four limbs and the skin, the vapor will spread throughout the body. After the vapor has made a complete circuit, it will be mature. Now the vapor will stir and rise again. When this happens, you must enter a state of true stillness. Once complete stillness is attained, the true vapor will be anchored, and its cycle of movement and stillness will follow the most subtle ways. When vapor is aroused, it should be kept safe within.

When it is still, the spirit will resonate with it. When the true vapor travels unhindered, your skin and complexion will be bright and clear, the nine cavities will be open, and the limbs will feel weightless. With time, the skin will take on the color of white jade.

3. Emergence of the Sacred Water

The sacred water is not the nectar of the Radiant Pool but the liquid that moistens the true vapor. In the north is a great sea, and within the great sea lives a mysterious tortoise. The mysterious tortoise exhales the true vapor, and the true vapor is transmuted into the sacred water. The sacred water gives birth to the kidney; this is why the sacred water is called the primal root of vapor. The vapor is inhaled and exhaled with the breath. When we breathe out, we push the vapor out an inch; when we breathe in, we take in one inch of vapor. If you minimize speech, thoughts, and physical movement, then one "foot" of vapor will grow every hour. During sleep, vapor also grows. If you dream, however, the mind will be active, and vapor will not be able to gather. Therefore in sleep, the spirit must also stop its activity. When there are no thoughts in sleep, there will be no dreams. When there are no dreams, the primal root will grow. Those who cultivate the Tao must stop their thoughts at midnight. Sit still, draw the vapor from the Celestial Pool (*t'ien-chih*) cavity, and let it swirl downward into the meridians. With time, the generative fluid will be plentiful. All methods of the art of longevity start here. First inhale from the Celestial Pool cavity, then channel the vapor into the Winding River, and finally let it swirl into the House of the Earth (*ti-wu*). If you accomplish these things, you will be free from hunger and thirst. The hundred channels will be nourished, and your body will be transformed in the most wondrous ways.

4. Circulating the True Fire

The true fire is not the fire of the heart. In the north is water, and it is within this water that the true fire is born. True fire is born in the north in the abyss of yin. Its light is reflected from the sun and can be collected in the following way. Clasp the hands together and move the fire around in the area of the waist. After the fire has crossed from one side of the body to the other, gather it in the lower elixir field. The fire will now begin to move like a snake. Zigzagging and spiraling up and down, it will leap around like a great flame. Moving naturally out of the kidneys, it will travel toward the shoulder blades. Then, thundering like a whirlwind, it will flow through the neck, enter the mouth, and exit from the nostrils. Next, the fire will penetrate the Celestial Gate and enter the Mudball cavity. Once it has reached the top of the head, the fire will become soft and warm. Pump it with your breath until you perspire. When the perspiration has purged all impurities, you will be able to stop aging and attain longevity. With continued practice, you will one day be able to fly up to the sky. These are all part of the wonderful experience of becoming an immortal.

5. The Infant Leaves the Womb

Refine the sun (the great yang) on the left, and the dragon will give birth to the fetus. Because water gives birth to wood, wood is regarded as the child of water. The vapor of water flows through the liquid. Thus, the green dragon is the vapor of wood. Within the green dragon is the one primordial vapor. It is from this vapor that the womb of the fetus is formed. When wood travels to the spleen, it is called the Yellow Woman. When the Yellow Woman nourishes the wood, the fetus will take on a greenish tint. People know the methods of visualization but do not understand the subtleties of applying it. While visualizing, you must also hold on to the vapor and use the four limbs to push it upward. Otherwise you won't be able to experience the great and subtle wonder.

6. The Young Woman Glows with Splendor

Refine the moon (the great yin) on the right, and the white tiger will give birth to the young woman. Because metal gives birth to water, metal is regarded as the mother of water. The vapor of metal flows through the water. Thus, the white tiger is the vapor of metal. Within the white tiger is the one primordial vapor. It is from this vapor that the womb of the young woman is formed. When metal travels to the kidneys, it will give birth to the child. Use the four limbs to move the vapor through the hundred circulatory pathways in the body. Let it swirl up, down, left, and right. If you hold on to the vapor and still the mind, the true body will emerge. Red and green hues will appear in front of you, sending rays of light to the four directions. In the gap between metal and wood, wood gives birth to fire and metal gives birth to water. The green dragon slows the vapor and directs the movement of fire. The white tiger strengthens the vapor and directs the movement of water.

When the two are set in motion, the effects are clear. This is the secret of the true immortals. Wait for the vapor to resonate with the mind. In seven days, you'll get the expected results.

7. *Copulation of Yin and Yang*

The yang within the yin is the supreme *essence* of yang and is called the splendor of the moon. The yin within the yang is the supreme spirit of yin and is called the *essence* of the sun. The supreme yang of the north gives birth to the waters of the kidneys. Within this water is yang fire. The supreme yin of the south gives birth to the fire of the heart. Within this fire is the yin water. When fire and water interact, their vapors will copulate and give birth to intelligent life forms. The true fire gives birth to lead, and the true water gives birth to mercury. When lead and mercury copulate, you will attain longevity. People today do not understand these subtleties. Therefore, they cannot experience the effects. You need to direct the vapor up to the Radiant Pool. Then, let it bubble up from the earth meridians and eventually descend to the island in the center of the heart. When the vapor rises in the spleen, the two primordial vapors will copulate, and you will feel as if you are intoxicated. The vapor will now circulate freely, and the hundred channels within will be harmonious. A thousand guardian spirits will visit you as you enter into a trance. The bones will be strong and supple, and your body will become like an infant's. With continued circulation of the vapor, the true body will emerge. Emanating as multiple forms, it can travel anywhere in the

realms of heaven and earth. Every realm in your internal universe will be numinous. This is the most subtle wonder.

SECTION TWO: REFINING THE MUNDANE TO OPEN THE
SACRED GATE

1. Light Emanates from the Sacred Body

The sacred body is born of the true gathering of the primordial
vapor. Still the spirit, cultivate simplicity, and with time the
sacred body will be refined. Once the sacred body is refined, it
will be surrounded by an aura of light. This is because the vapor
resonates with generative energy; the generative energy resonates with the spirit; and the spirit resonates with the body.
These three wondrous things must now be circulated up, down,
and around within. Use the fire to refine the vapor so that the
vapor can rise to penetrate the hundred circulatory pathways
and enter the hundred cavities. At night, in stillness you will
see five-colored clouds enveloping you and feel as if you are
submerged in fire. These phenomena will happen only when
the three energies are locked inside and the vapor is circulating.
When vapor circulates, the generative energy will become
strong. When generative energy is strong, it will preserve the
spirit. When the spirit becomes numinous, it will naturally send
its light out of the body. As the glow of the light spreads to the
four directions, the vapor's wind will beat about within and
vapor will swirl around ceaselessly. With time, the vapor will
emanate from the body, bathing it in a soft light. With continued practice, the glow will be transformed into five-colored

clouds. Stepping on these clouds, you will be able to enter the celestial realm.

2. *The Five Viscera Become Clear and Bright*

The five viscera are the source of the five elements (in the body). After the five elements have been refined, you should hold on to the vapor. To hold on to the vapor is to focus on its movement in the body. Let it swirl left and right, always keeping it circulating. When all blockages are open, your body will be protected and preserved, and you will be free from hunger and thirst. Blood and vapor will merge, spirit will become clear and numinous, and you will be transformed into an immortal. Such are the wonders of the subtle teachings. These then are the keys to cultivation: circulating the vapor is the foundation; focusing and emptying the mind constitute the supreme teachings; closing the orifices is the catalyst; and the Mudball cavity is where cultivation comes to fruition. In practice, first close the orifices and focus the mind. While focusing the mind, circulate the vapor. As vapor rises from the (lower) elixir field, churn it around. Finally, direct the vapor to the four limbs when you feel the vapor stir in the heart. In this way, the vapors within the five viscera will communicate with one another, and you will be free from illness. If the vapors of the five viscera are harmonious, your complexion will glow with brightness. If you see the five-colored gems when you gaze within, it is a sign that the process of cultivation is complete. Circulate the vapors for a period of time, and the light from within will merge with that of the five stars.

3. The Four Body Components Are Nourished Internally

Every person has these four bodily components: externally there are the skin and muscles; internally there are the bones and blood. If you empty the mind of thoughts, you will become an enlightened being. However, in order for the body to ascend to the sky, you must first nourish the four bodily components. Follow these instructions carefully. Sit upright and keep your body still. Cross the legs and place your palms against each other. Let the heat penetrate the five viscera. Vapor flowing from the hands will first interact with the area of the spine between the shoulder blades. Next, vapor from the legs will interact with the area of the spine below the waist. Shake the upper and lower parts of the body until the four limbs are covered in perspiration. Once the impurities are purged through perspiring, thousands of ailments will go away and hundreds of afflictions will cease. At this point, you will no longer be plagued by illnesses or injuries. Those who cultivate themselves must therefore learn to circulate the vapor without delay.

4. The Three Palaces Glow with a Yellow Light

The method of holding on to the One was given to humanity by the celestial beings. It is said that the Yellow Emperor was the first to receive these teachings. First, get the vapor to rise from the lower elixir field. When the vapor's strength is at its height, fire from the heart will emerge and sink to interact with the vapor in the navel. Next, when the middle elixir field is activated, hold on to the One and still the spirit. Third, when cultivating the upper elixir field, be sure to direct the Jade

Essence down and swallow it into the Radiant Pool cavity. Otherwise, the true essence will not enter the heart. With continued practice, sight and hearing will be enhanced. When the vapor flows down and penetrates the kidneys, the sacred fire will ascend. The three palaces will now glow with a yellow light forming the Yellow Path. Practice these techniques diligently, and you will be able to fly to the sky, become omniscient, and never age. These are the complete teachings of the Yellow Emperor.

5. The Sacred Fire Enters the Cauldron

Those who cultivate the mind must use vapor as the metal to make the cauldron. The cauldron is located below the spleen and above the waist. Inside the cauldron is the pill. The pill is the product of the two vapors of *k'an* and *li* copulating within the spleen. Inside the cauldron is also water. This water is the primordial vapor. The primordial vapor will not rise if there is no fire. Fire is ignited from below, and this fire is the fire within the water in the palace of *k'an*. It is also called the sacred fire, the yang within the yin, and the essence of the sun. When the light of the pill radiates upward, the pill can be circulated using the appropriate method. When the pill materializes, swallow it into the Radiant Pool together with three hundred mouthfuls of the true saliva. Then, each morning at sunrise, visualize the essence of the sun and swallow the saliva 360 times. Finally, activate the stored essence at midnight to steam the pill, which is now merged with the essence of the sun.

6. The Light of the Pill Resonates with the Fluid

The pill tempers the spirit. It is the precious substance of the supreme yang. When the pill strengthens the hundred channels internally and penetrates the nine cavities externally, the sacred light will shine and the fluid will flow. Inside, the sacred spring will be filled, moistening and nourishing the body. Outside, the vapor of supreme harmony will be transformed into fluid, manifesting as perspiration soaking the body. When you reach this stage of cultivation, no illness will arise. Your body will become light, and with time it will be bathed in a pure light. Your gait will be swift, and you will be able to run up the mountain paths. Nothing can stop you because you are now protected by the bright spirit.

7. The Jade Spring Does Not Dissipate

The Jade Spring (*yü-chuan*) is the location where the true generative essence emerges. Those who have cultivated it for a long time will attain it. Once you have realized the Jade Spring within, you will need to start these three processes: first, reverse the flow in the Mudball cavity; second, empty all thoughts from the abode of the spirit; third, lock the true primordial vapor within. Once these processes are activated, the generative essence will emerge, flowing endlessly like a gushing spring that feeds a river. The source of this river, however, never leaves the mountain valley where it emerges. If you have reached this stage of cultivation, how can the mind be stirred? How can there be leakage? The casual practitioner does not know that the procedures described above are crucial to activating the Jade Spring. Those who have activated the Jade Spring will always be nourished within, for the Jade Spring cannot be exhausted. The keys to this method are: stilling the spirit, cultivating the vapor and letting it rise to the Mudball cavity, and strengthening the vapor so that it does not dissipate.

SECTION THREE: CULTIVATING THE MUNDANE FORM TO GENERATE MULTIPLE FORMS

1. Preserving the Spirit and Giving Birth to the Fetus

The spirit is born from the fetus, and the fetus is born of life energy. When the fetus is conceived, the spirit emerges. When life energy grows, it will take on a form. This is because vapor energizes vapor and spirit itself creates spirit. When the source of the vapor is activated, the energy of the source will become smooth and harmonious. However, if the mind is attached to desire and appearances, the source will be stirred and shaken, and the spirit will be injured. Strain the body, and the spirit will be harmed. If 30 percent of the spirit is taxed, the spirit will suffer. If 50 percent of the mind is occupied, the spirit will be hurt. If 70 percent of your life is under strain, the spirit will be wounded severely. A wayward mind taxes the body; desire for sensual pleasure and attachment to things drain the vapor. Anxiety and worry strain the mind. The amount of injury done to the spirit will vary among people. The enlightened ones know the importance of preserving the spirit and conserving generative energy. Thus, their bodies are healthy and their spirits are clear. If you have difficulty in attaining stillness, you can use ginseng to temper the three palaces. Live a life with little excitement and activity. Regulate your food and drink. Do not expose the body to extreme cold or heat. Rise and sleep at regular hours. Do not let routines control your life, and do not be a prisoner of social conventions. If you live this lifestyle, you will be able to cultivate the fetus and the spirit. The fetus is the product of returning to simplicity. It is through simplicity that the spirit is nurtured. After you have attained simplicity, you can then practice the method of stilling the spirit.

2. *Preserving the Vapor and the True Source*

In nourishing the vapor, you need to protect the body and strengthen life energy. To nurture the primordial vapor and nourish the ultimate reality within, you need to minimize thinking and break your attachment to desire. Those with weak bodies should first use herbs (for example, the yellow essence of chrysanthemum) to strengthen their constitution. Next, they should practice the methods of circulating the primordial vapor to nourish generative and vital energy. Only then can they hope to cultivate the fetus. If you practice the techniques correctly, the vapor will become strong and plentiful, and the true source will emerge. The true source is that which gives birth to life. All methods of cultivating the Tao come from these principles.

3. *Flying, Running, and Climbing Effortlessly*

The key to becoming an immortal lies in the transformation of the spirit. The ability to fly, run, and climb effortlessly comes from possessing a spirit body. When muscles and tendons are strong and the breath is deep, the body will become light and agile, and the spirit body will glow with radiance. If you want to have strong muscles and tendons, you must still the mind and nourish the blood. Practice calisthenics or self-massage. At midnight, regulate your breath and focus on the green dragon emerging from the kidneys. Next, direct the vapor of the green dragon to the waist and the four limbs. Finally, let it rise to the cavity of the Celestial Gate. Swallow the true nectar from the Radiant Pool nine times. Recite seven times the mantra that petitions the celestial powers to help you in your cultivation. If you want to develop endurance, you will need to conserve generative energy. If you want the body to become light and agile, you should practice the methods of cultivating the generative, vital, and spirit energies.

4. The Steps of Yü the Great

Yü the Great had power over the hundred spirits. This was because he knew how to dance the steps of the celestial year. If you dance the steps of the celestial year, you will be able to escape these three destructive forces: thunder in the sky and lightning striking the earth; evil spirits inhabiting the mountains and rivers; and poisonous snakes and insects. Those who cultivate the Tao must be able to overcome these dangers. If you know the pattern of the celestial steps, you can climb to the clouds and wander in the three realms. No matter where you go, the immortals will protect you. Use the steps of Yü when you ascend the altar to make sky offerings. Dance the steps before you enter deep into the mountains. First, tap the teeth together to produce a series of clicking sounds. Next, close your eyes and visualize the sun and moon. Now you can begin the dance. Extend the right arm along the north-south axis. Make a fist with the left hand leaving the second finger extended. Walk toward the east. When you step with the right foot, the finger should be pointing to the southeast, and you should be facing the east. Next, make a fist with the right hand, again leaving the second finger extended. Now, take a step with the left foot. The finger should be pointing to the northeast, and again you should be facing and walking toward the east. Make sure the guardians of the three realms are present before you begin to dance the steps.

5. *Taming Spirits and Ghosts*

The enlightened ones have the power to command and tame mischievous spirits. Their power comes from their cultivation, and their strength is founded on discipline. When they encounter evil ghosts and spirits, they can use their power to tame them. And, in doing so, they are promoted and become officers of the celestial realm. If you want to drive away evil apparitions, you must first perform the purification rites. Then recite the appropriate petitions to the celestial powers. Finally, use nine ounces of cinnabar to open the channels between the three realms, and use dough to fashion the likeness of the true form. Take one thousand sheets of green and white paper and burn them under a pine tree. When you see green and white clouds hovering above the tree, the malevolent spirits will naturally leave.

6. Projecting the Spirit and Transforming into Multiple Forms

The true spirit exists along with the mind of desire and emotions. Everyone has the true spirit, but for most people, the true spirit is dominated by desire and emotions. Thus, their spirits are imprisoned within the body. The enlightened ones, however, are able to project their spirit outside the body to communicate with others. In life, they can enter another person's dreams. After death, the spirit can "borrow" a corporeal form for habitation. When cultivation is complete, the spirit will be still and no longer wayward and mischievous. The Celestial Gate will open, and the spirit will be able to exit. This is how the enlightened ones send messages to others through dreams, take on corporeal form, and appear as apparitions in broad daylight. Those with cluttered minds and weak vapor and those who are intoxicated are most likely to be frightened by these apparitions.

7. Helping Nonsentient Beings

When the spirit walks with you, things around you will be transformed by the power of the ultimate reality. Things that do not have compassion, such as those that live in the water, will become sentient when they are near the spirit of enlightened beings. In the same manner, inanimate objects like rocks can become sentient spirits. Mountains and rivers, rocks and trees can benefit from the presence of immortal beings. Receiving the vapor of the enlightened ones, they can develop compassion. As a result, not only will they not harm people, but they will do good and kind deeds, thus helping people as well as accumulating merit for themselves.